Deploying Microsoft® Forefront® Unified Access Gateway 2010

Yuri Diogenes
Dr. Thomas W. Shinder

PUBLISHED BY
Microsoft Press
A Division of Microsoft Corporation
One Microsoft Way
Redmond, Washington 98052-6399

Library of Congress Control Number: 2010938149

Printed and bound in the United States of America.

Microsoft Press books are available through booksellers and distributors worldwide. For further information about international editions, contact your local Microsoft Corporation office or contact Microsoft Press International directly at fax (425) 936-7329. Visit our Web site at www.microsoft.com/mspress. Send comments to mspinput@ microsoft.com.

Acquisitions Editor: Devon Musgrave
Developmental Editor: Karen Szall
Project Editor: Karen Szall
Editorial Production: nSight, Inc.
Technical Reviewer: Mitch Tulloch; Technical Review services provided by Content Master, a member of CM Group, Ltd.
Cover: Tom Draper Design

Body Part No. X17-15049

Contents

Introduction   ix

Chapter 1   Understanding Forefront Unified Access Gateway   1

    From IAG to Forefront UAG 1

    What's New in Forefront UAG 4

        Improvements for Installation and Deployment   5

        High Availability and Scalability   6

        UAG as a DirectAccess Server   7

        New Publishing Capabilities   8

        Remote Access Client VPN Services   9

        Other New Features   9

    When to Use Forefront UAG 12

    Administrator's Punch List 13

Chapter 2   Planning and Installing Forefront UAG   15

    Planning Forefront UAG Deployment 15

        Corporate Access Model   16

        Name Resolution   17

        Public Key Infrastructure   18

        Domain and Workgroup Membership   19

        IPv6 Considerations   20

        External and Internal Firewalls   21

        Fault Tolerance and Load Balancing   24

        Network Access Protection   24

    Hardware Requirements 26

What do you think of this book? We want to hear from you!

Microsoft is interested in hearing your feedback so we can continually improve our books and learning resources for you. To participate in a brief online survey, please visit:

www.microsoft.com/learning/booksurvey/

Software Requirements 26
    Forefront UAG Server Software Requirements   26
    Forefront UAG Client Requirements   27

Installing Forefront UAG 29

Configuring Forefront UAG 34

Deploying a Forefront UAG Array 43
    Requirements   43
    Creating an Array   43

Administrator's Punch List 48

Chapter 3   **Publishing Applications through Forefront UAG**   **51**

Understanding the Publishing Mechanism on Forefront UAG 51
    Authentication Repository   52
    Creating a Portal Trunk   55
    Client Experience   60

Publishing Exchange 63

Publishing Remote Desktop Services 71
    Why Use Forefront UAG to Publish Remote Desktop Services?   73
    Publishing RemoteApp Programs   74
    Publishing an Administrator-Controlled Remote Desktop   79
    Publishing User-Defined Desktops   82

Publishing SharePoint 85
    Why Use Forefront UAG as a SharePoint Publishing Solution?   86
    Forefront UAG Web Site Certificate Requirements   87
    Publishing a Simple Windows SharePoint Services 3.0
    Web Site   88
    Validating the Configuration   90

Administrator's Punch List 94

Chapter 4   **Implementing SSL VPN with Forefront UAG**   **95**

Understanding SSL VPN Options 95

Planning and Configuring SSTP 96
    Configuring SSTP on Forefront UAG   99

Client Experience with SSTP   102

Configuring SSL Network Tunneling 102

    Customizing Network Connector Settings   109

    Client Experience with Network Connector   111

Administrator's Punch List.......................................113

Chapter 5   Implementing Forefront UAG with DirectAccess   115

How DirectAccess Works 116

    DirectAccess Client Connectivity   117

    IPv6 Transition Technologies   119

    The Name Resolution Policy Table (NRPT)   121

    Forefront UAG NAT64/DNS64 and IPv4-Only
    Corporate Resources   123

    Infrastructure Components of a Forefront UAG
    DirectAccess Solution   125

    DirectAccess Security Considerations   132

    Summary of the DirectAccess Client Security Model   140

Forefront UAG 2010 DirectAccess Requirements 141

Forefront UAG 2010 DirectAccess Configuration Wizard 142

    Running the Forefront UAG DirectAccess Wizard   142

Administrator's Punch List.......................................153

What do you think of this book? We want to hear from you!

Microsoft is interested in hearing your feedback so we can continually improve our books and learning resources for you. To participate in a brief online survey, please visit:

www.microsoft.com/learning/booksurvey/

Acknowledgments

This Forefront project took almost a year to write and resulted in three separate books about deploying Forefront products. Although the authors get lots of credit, there can be little doubt that we could not have even begun, much less completed, this book without the cooperation (not to mention the permission) of an incredibly large number of people.

It's here that we'd like to take a few moments of your time to express our gratitude to the folks who made it all possible.

With thanks...

To the folks at Microsoft Press who made the process as smooth as they possibly could: Karen Szall, Devon Musgrave, and their crew.

To the UAG Product Team folks, especially Meir Mendelovich, Olga Shoikhet, Nathan Bigman, and all of the UAG Technical Writers. To the UAG CSS Team, especially Dan Herzog, Tarun Sachdeva, Ben Ari, Dan Watson, and Mike Havens. Also, I can't forget our buddy Uri Lichtenfeld, who continues to help the team.

From Yuri

First and foremost to God, for blessing my life, leading my way, and giving me the strength to take on the challenges as just another step in life. To my eternal supporter in all moments of my life: my wife Alexsandra. To my daughters who, although very young, understand when I close the office door and say, "I'm really busy." Thanks for understanding. I love you, Yanne and Ysis.

To my friend Thomas Shinder, whom I was fortunate enough to meet three years ago. Thanks for shaping my writing skills and also contributing to my personal grown with your thoughts, advice, and guidance. Without a doubt, these long months working on this project were worth it because of our amazing partnership. I can't forget to thank the two other friends who wrote the *Microsoft Forefront Threat Management Gateway Administrator's Companion* with me: Jim Harrison and Mohit Saxena. They were, without a doubt, the pillars for this writing career in which I'm now fully engaged. Thanks, guys.

To, as Jim says, "da Boyz": Tim "Thor" Mullen, Steve Moffat, and Greg Mulholland. You guys are amazing. Thanks for sharing all the tales. To all Forefront MVPs, especially my MVP friends Richard Hicks, Alberto Oliveira, and Airton Leal, keep up the great work and keep pushing us to write more. Last, but not least, to all the CSS folks in EMEA who are supporting UAG; you guys, indeed, inspired us to keep writing.

From Tom

As Yuri does, I acknowledge the blessings from God, who took "a fool like me" and guided me on a path that I never would have chosen on my own. The second most important acknowledgement I must make is to my beautiful wife, Deb Shinder, whom I consider my hand of God. Without her, I don't know where I would be today, except that I know that the place wouldn't be anywhere near as good as the place I am now.

I also want to acknowledge my good friend Yuri Diogenes, my co-writer in this project. Yuri really held this project together. I had just started working for Microsoft and was learning about the ins and outs of the Microsoft system, and I was also taking on a lot of detailed and complex projects alongside the writing of this book. Yuri helped keep me focused, spent a lot of time pointing me in the right direction, and essentially is responsible for enabling me to get done what I needed to get done. I have no doubt that, without Yuri guiding this effort, it probably never would have been completed.

Props go out to Jim Harrison, "the King of TMG" and heir apparent to UAG, as well as to Greg Mulholland, Steve Moffat, and Tim Mullen. You guys were the moral authority that drove us to completion. I also want to give a special "shout out" to Ben Bernstein, Yaniv Naor, John Morello, Pat Telford, and Billy Price. These "five horsemen" of UAG DirectAccess provided me with insights and understanding of UAG DirectAccess that very few people can deliver, and I was the beneficiary, time after time, of their unique skills in this area.

I also want to thank Uri Lichtenfeld, the face of IAG and UAG for so many years. Uri has been a great friend and confidante over the years, and his insights into UAG really helped me understand not only the "hows," but also the "whys" that underpin UAG features and functionality.

Also, I couldn't have done this without my team, led by Nathan Bigman. As Yuri did, I benefited from Nathan's undying patience with the way I do my work. Without his guidance and leadership, I couldn't have completed this project.

Finally, I want to give thanks to the operators of ISAserver.org and all the members of the ISAserver.org community. You guys were the spark that started a flaming hot career for me with ISA Server and then TMG. You guys are a never-ending inspiration and a demonstration of the power of community and the ways communities can work together to solve hard problems and share solutions.

Introduction

When we began this project, our intent was to create a real-world scenario that would guide IT professionals in using Microsoft best practices to deploy Microsoft Forefront Unified Access Gateway (UAG) 2010. We also included an explanation of the architectural side of the product, which we consider an advantage for you, because the explanation was reviewed by engineers who work directly on UAG at Microsoft Customer Service and Support (CSS). This book provides administrative procedures, tested design examples, quick answers, and tips. In addition, it covers some of the most common deployment scenarios and describes ways to take full advantage of the product's capabilities. This book covers pre-deployment tasks, software and hardware requirements, performance considerations, and installation and configuration, using best practice recommendations.

Who Is This Book For?

Deploying Microsoft Forefront Unified Access Gateway 2010 covers Forefront UAG deployment in a number of scenarios. This book is designed for:

- Administrators who are deploying Forefront UAG
- Administrators who are experienced with Windows Server 2008 R2 and Microsoft Forefront Threat Management Gateway (TMG)
- Current Forefront UAG administrators
- Administrators who are new to Forefront UAG
- Technology specialists, such as network administrators and security administrators

Because this book is limited in size and we want to provide you the maximum value, we assume a basic knowledge of Windows Server 2008 R2, Active Directory Domain and Certificate Services, and Windows networking. These technologies are not discussed in detail, but this book contains material on all of these topics that relates to Forefront UAG administrative tasks.

How Is This Book Organized?

Deploying Microsoft Forefront Unified Access Gateway 2010 is written to be a deployment guide and to serve as a source of architectural information related to the product. The book is organized in such a way that you can follow the steps to plan and deploy the product; the steps are based on a deployment scenario for the company Contoso. As you go through the steps you will also notice tips for best practice implementation. At the end of each chapter, you will see an "Administrator's Punch List," in which you will find a summary of the main administrative tasks that were covered throughout the chapter. This is a quick checklist to help you review the main deployment tasks.

The book is organized into five chapters:

- Chapter 1, "Understanding Forefront Unified Access Gateway"
- Chapter 2, "Planning and Installing Forefront UAG"
- Chapter 3, "Publishing Applications through Forefront UAG"
- Chapter 4, "Implementing SSL VPN with Forefront UAG"
- Chapter 5, "Implementing Forefront UAG with DirectAccess"

We hope you find *Deploying Microsoft Forefront Unified Access Gateway 2010* useful and accurate. We have an open door policy for e-mail at *mspress .uagbook@tacteam.net*, and you can contact us through our personal blogs and follow us on our Twitter accounts:

- *http://blogs.technet.com/yuridiogenes* and *http://blogs.technet.com /tomshinder*
- *http://twitter.com/yuridiogenes* and *http://twitter.com/tshinder*

Support for This Book

Every effort has been made to ensure the accuracy of this book. As corrections or changes are collected, they will be added the O'Reilly Media website. To find Microsoft Press book and media corrections:

1. Go to *http://microsoftpress.oreilly.com*.
2. In the Search box, type the ISBN for the book, and click Search.
3. Select the book from the search results, which will take you to the book's catalog page.
4. On the book's catalog page, under the picture of the book cover, click View/Submit Errata.

If you have questions regarding the book or the companion content that are not answered by visiting the book's catalog page, please send them to Microsoft Press by sending an email message to *mspinput@microsoft.com*.

We Want to Hear from You

We welcome your feedback about this book. Please share your comments and ideas through the following short survey:

http://www.microsoft.com/learning/booksurvey

Your participation helps Microsoft Press create books that better meet your needs and your standards.

> **NOTE** We hope that you will give us detailed feedback in our survey. If you have questions about our publishing program, upcoming titles, or Microsoft Press in general, we encourage you to interact with us using Twitter at *http://twitter.com/MicrosoftPress*. For support issues, use only the email address shown earlier.

CHAPTER 1

Understanding Forefront Unified Access Gateway

▪ From IAG to Forefront UAG   **1**

▪ What's New in Forefront UAG   **4**

▪ When to Use Forefront UAG   **12**

M icrosoft Forefront Unified Access Gateway (UAG) 2010 is the evolution of the Microsoft Intelligent Application Gateway (IAG). Forefront UAG preserves the core capabilities of its predecessor, and it adds enhancements that make this version of the product a more robust and transparent solution for inbound access from anywhere. When deployed in a corporate scenario, Forefront UAG helps to provide employees, partners, and customers with seamless secure access to almost any application from almost any device. This chapter covers the history of Forefront UAG, describes the new features in this version, and explains when this product should be used.

From IAG to Forefront UAG

Originally, IAG was called Whale; it was a product of Whale Communications, a company that Microsoft acquired in 2006. While IAG was capable of implementing a powerful portal with customization capabilities and a Secure Sockets Layer Virtual Private Network (SSL VPN), it was initially offered only through OEM partners as an appliance-based solution.

IAG 2007 included components that were not present in the original Whale product. One of the main additions was ISA Server 2006 Standard Edition, as a local firewall, to protect IAG 2007 against attacks coming from both internal and external interfaces. While this added more value to the product, having ISA Server 2006 pre-installed on IAG 2007 caused some misinterpretation about the final goal, and ISA 2006 was used for other purposes (such as publishing applications) that were not recommended by Microsoft. Over time, Microsoft clarified the supportability boundaries between IAG and ISA, so that administrators could take full advantage of both products. Figure 1-1 shows the core IAG 2007 components.

| IAG 2007 |
| IIS 6 |
| ISA Server 2006 |
| Windows Server 2003 |

FIGURE 1-1

> **NOTE** For more information on the IAG 2007 architecture, read Chapter 2, "What Are the Differences between TMG and UAG," in *Microsoft Forefront Threat Management Gateway (TMG) Administrator's Companion* from Microsoft Press.

Forefront UAG not only offers new capabilities, but also changes the platform to be natively 64-bit, running on Windows Server 2008 R2, with Microsoft Forefront Threat Management Gateway (TMG) 2010 as a firewall, so it can be an edge-ready device. Forefront UAG has a new architecture that takes advantage of new components available on Windows Server 2008. Figure 1-2 shows the Forefront UAG architecture:

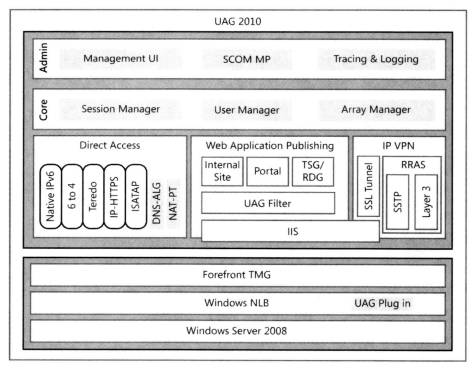

FIGURE 1-2

As you can see in Figure 1-2, there are many new components in Forefront UAG. Some of them, such as DirectAccess, Windows Network Load Balancing (NLB), and Secure Socket Tunneling Protocol (SSTP), are inherited through integration with the Windows Server 2008 R2 platform. The new components are:

- **Management UI**   The management user interface is the UAG console for managing either a single server or an array.
- **SCOM MP**   This is the management package for the Microsoft System Center Operations Manager that can be used for UAG.
- **Tracing and Logging**   These components are used for troubleshooting.
- **Session Manager**   This is the component responsible for managing a session on UAG.
- **User Manager**   This component is responsible for managing a user's authentication and authorization on UAG.
- **Array Manager**   This new addition to UAG allows management of more than one server in an array infrastructure.
- **DirectAccess Components**   These are the Windows DirectAccess components that are used by UAG.
- **Web Application Publishing**   These are UAG components that handle general Web application publishing. The UAG Filter (whlfilter.dll) is the component that runs on top of IIS.
- **IIS**   Internet Information Server 7 is built-in on Windows Server 2008 R2 and is used as the core platform for UAG.
- **IP VPN**   These components are used for remote access VPN. UAG uses HTTP.SYS as a kernel-mode component for SSL Tunnel and uses Routing and Remote Access (RRAS) components for SSTP and Layer 3 filtering.
- **Forefront TMG**   Forefront TMG 2010 is used to protect UAG itself and to provide other services to UAG.
- **Windows NLB**   UAG uses Windows NLB services for load balancing and hooks up a UAG plug-in to manage these services.
- **Windows Server 2008**   This is the operating system used by UAG.

> **NOTE**   There are more details about UAG integration with DirectAccess in Chapter 5, "Implementing DirectAccess with UAG."

Using the same approach that was used in the IAG 2007 life cycle, Microsoft decided to make Forefront UAG available in different deployment packages, to provide more flexibility to customers who want to test Forefront UAG before they deploy it. Table 1-1 shows the deployment options that are available in Forefront UAG:

TABLE 1-1 TMG distribution options

OPTION	UAG/TMG	OPERATING SYSTEM
Commercial software	Enterprise Edition	Requires that you install the software on your own hardware, and that you have, as a minimum, Windows Server 2008 R2 Standard Edition or Enterprise Edition
OEM	Enterprise Edition	Installed by the OEM on OEM hardware; requires, as a minimum, Windows Server 2008 R2 Standard Edition or Enterprise Edition
Evaluation	Enterprise Edition (120-day trial)	Requires that you install the software on your own hardware, and that you have, as a minimum, Windows Server 2008 R2 Standard Edition or Enterprise Edition
Commercial VHD	Enterprise Edition	Requires that you have Windows Server 2008 R2 Standard Edition

What's New in Forefront UAG

IAG 2007 was a good start and provided a robust SSL VPN solution that included socket and port forwarding, as well as a Network Connector. When IAG was introduced, it was intended to provide only these basic SSL VPN services. The development of UAG introduced a new role for the solution: not only to provide basic remote access SSL VPN service, but to become the single, unified access gateway for all remote access connections to a corporate network. By using a single remote access solution for a variety of remote access connectivity options, UAG could provide a single console, a single point of configuration, a single point of logging and reporting, and a single point of troubleshooting.

To provide this unified remote access solution, Forefront UAG needs to support many more remote access connectivity methods than just those provided by an SSL VPN solution. Specifically, Forefront UAG also provides support for:

- Secure Sockets Tunneling Protocol (SSTP) remote access VPN client connections.
- Hosting a Remote Desktop Gateway on the UAG server itself.
- DirectAccess, a new remote access solution that enables a corporate network computing experience for users located anywhere on the Internet.

This combination of remote access connectivity options enhances the prior SSL-VPN-only solution provided by IAG. With UAG, you can customize the type of remote access experience users have by enabling different remote access connectivity options. For example, users who require access to one or two applications can use the SSL VPN feature in UAG. Users who require more comprehensive access to corporate network resources, but who connect from unmanaged machines, can take advantage of the SSTP network layer VPN option. And users running domain-member, managed computers can use the new DirectAccess solution for a completely corporate-network-like end-user experience when connecting to organizational resources.

There are many other features and capabilities built into UAG that weren't available in IAG. These fall into the following categories and are described in the sections that follow:

- Installation and deployment improvements
- High availability and scalability
- DirectAccess server capability
- New publishing features
- Remote access client VPN services

Improvements for Installation and Deployment

Changes in installation and deployment are seen in:

- 64-bit software installation
- Support for virtual machine deployments
- Changes in the built-in firewall
- An improved Getting Started Wizard

64-Bit Software Installation

IAG was a 32-bit application that ran on Windows Server 2003. Forefront UAG is a native 64-bit application that runs only on Windows Server 2008 R2. The upgrade to a native 64-bit application helps ensure that UAG is more stable, more secure, and more scalable than IAG could be, due to the limitations of the 32-bit architecture on which IAG was built.

A Pre-Configured Virtual Appliance Option

IAG SP2 was the first version of IAG that was available in a .vhd file format. However, its utility in this format was limited, and full support was not clearly defined for the virtual deployment. UAG allows you to purchase the product in one of several ways. You can obtain a fully-built UAG appliance for any of a number of UAG OEMs; you can purchase the UAG software and install it on your own systems; or you can get a virtual appliance, which is a pre-configured .vhd that you can run on Windows Server 2008 R2 and above, with the Hyper-V role installed. This is an important advance, because virtualization is seeing an increasing presence in the data center, and it is likely that one of the prime candidates for virtualization is a secure remote access solution such as UAG.

Enhanced Host-based and Network Firewall

IAG used the ISA firewall as a host-based and network-level firewall. The ISA server components were installed on the machine that had IAG software installed. The ISA firewall protected the IAG server itself from attack from both external and internal threats. This is a critical distinction, because most industry security analysts consider attacks from inside the firewall to be as important and as destructive as those that come from the outside.

UAG uses the latest version of the ISA firewall as its host-based and network-level firewall. However, the ISA firewall is now named Forefront TMG 2010. Forefront TMG provides even more robust protection from external attack than the ISA firewall provided, because it includes new security enhancements, such as the Network Inspection System, and a more robust 64-bit architecture. The Forefront TMG firewall also protects the UAG server from attack by internal or external intruders. Forefront TMG has several important additional features, such as the SSTP remote access VPN server component and the NAT64 Internet Protocol version 6 and Internet Protocol version 4 (IPv6/IPv4) protocol translators, all of which are available to Forefront UAG.

Getting Started Wizard

Setting up the IAG server was a bit difficult, because you needed to do planning and configuration of the Windows Server operating system before you could get the IAG components working. However, this wasn't a major issue for the majority of IAG users, because they could only get the product from an IAG server OEM vendor, and it came pre-installed and pre-configured.

This had to change with UAG, because UAG can be purchased as a software-only solution. Therefore, UAG includes a new Getting Started Wizard that walks you through the process of configuring the network interfaces, defining the internal network, configuring UAG arrays, and setting itself up to use Microsoft Update for Operating Systems and UAG application updates.

High Availability and Scalability

Two areas in which Forefront UAG improves on high availability and scalability are:

- **Multi-Server Arrays with UAG** You can create UAG arrays with up to eight members. Array configuration is stored in an Active Directory Lightweight Directory Services (AD LDS) database. A single server is designated as the Array Management Server (AMS), and configuration changes are made only on that server. Configuration changes made on the AMS are then automatically deployed to all other array members, thus ensuring that configuration is centralized and that all machines in the array have the same configuration.

- **Network Load Balancing** UAG provides built-in support for Network Load Balancing, with an integrated, easy to use wizard to configure it. Although Forefront TMG supports both unicast and multicast modes, Forefront UAG Network Load

Balancing supports only unicast mode. Network Load Balancing is also supported by Microsoft Hyper-V Server 2008 and later, so you can use NLB for UAG arrays that are hosted in a virtual deployment.

UAG as a DirectAccess Server

DirectAccess is a new remote access technology, included in Windows Sever 2008 R2, that allows users to connect to the corporate network without establishing a traditional network-level VPN connection. When a user connects from a DirectAccess-enabled client system, the computing experience is exactly the same as it is for a user who is directly connected to the corporate network over a wired or wireless connection. The user is able to connect to file servers, database servers, mail servers, collaboration servers, and any other servers you can think of, in the same way that users on the corporate network do. All this happens in the background. You do not need to do anything to establish the DirectAccess connection to the corporate network.

Another exciting feature of DirectAccess is the ability to remotely manage DirectAccess clients located on the Internet. In contrast to remote access VPN, SSL VPN, or reverse proxy remote access solutions, enterprise IT has the ability to manage the DirectAccess clients in the same way that it manages any other managed host on the corporate network. This means that you can use System Center Configuration Manager, System Center Operations Manager, Active Directory Group Policy, and almost any other systems management solution to manage DirectAccess clients, so that they always remain within the terms dictated by corporate compliance mandates.

In addition, DirectAccess supports smart card authentication and NAP network access control. Users can be forced to use two-factor authentication smart cards and can also be required to pass NAP security tests before being allowed access to the corporate network, in the same way that clients that attempt to connect to the corporate network over a wired or wireless connection must pass security tests.

DirectAccess is part of Windows Server 2008 R2 and Windows 7. Both are required for a DirectAccess solution. However, the Windows-only approach to DirectAccess is somewhat limited, in that there is no built-in support for NLB, no array support, and no support for non-IPv6 resources on the corporate network.

In contrast, using Forefront UAG adds the following features to a Windows DirectAccess solution:

- Support for DirectAccess array deployment, so that you can deploy an array of Forefront UAG DirectAccess servers to provide high availability.
- Support for Network Load Balancing, so that the array can always be available as long as one server in the NLB cluster is running.
- Support for network access to IPv4-only servers through the implementation of the DNS64 and NAT64 technologies. These technologies allow DirectAccess clients to

connect to legacy Windows 2000 Server and Windows Server 2003 server resources that are not IPv6-aware.

DirectAccess is one of the key scenarios supported by UAG, and it converts the Windows-based DirectAccess solution to an enterprise-ready, access-anywhere solution for domain-member-managed clients in your organization.

New Publishing Capabilities

IAG was the thought leader when it came to secure Web publishing for core line of business applications. Publishing support features now included with UAG are:

- Client/server application publishing
- Publishing Exchange Web services
- Publishing SharePoint Web services
- Publishing Remote Desktop Services
- Web Farm Load Balancing

In addition to the overview provided in this section, you'll also find detailed information about the publishing capabilities in Chapter 3, "Publishing Applications through UAG."

Client/Server Application Publishing

With client/server application publishing, you can publish non-Web applications to users on the Internet. Client/server application publishing allows you to connect your users to services, such as Exchange servers, using the native MAPI/RPC protocols. This type of publishing is accomplished using port and socket forwarding, which requires a lightweight client applica-tion that is installed from the UAG portal itself. A number of client/server applications are included out of the box, so you do not need to figure out what protocols are required to get remote access over an SSL VPN connection working.

Exchange Services Publishing

Forefront UAG includes full support for publishing Exchange Web services for Exchange Server 2003 and Exchange 2007 and Exchange 2010. Using built-in application optimizers, you can publish Outlook Web Access, Outlook Web App, Exchange ActiveSync, and Outlook Anywhere (RPC/HTTP).

SharePoint Publishing

Forefront UAG also includes full support for publishing SharePoint 2003, SharePoint 2007, and SharePoint 2010. Application optimizers are updated for each version of SharePoint to help ensure that intelligent application layer inspection is performed on all connections to SharePoint, so they are secure when made through the UAG SSL VPN gateway.

Remote Desktop Gateway Publishing

Completely new in UAG is the ability to host a Remote Desktop Gateway solution on the Forefront UAG server itself. Integrated and easy to use wizards are included so that you can quickly and easily set up the Remote Desktop Gateway to get a working solution in record time. There are a number of advantages to having the Forefront UAG server host your RD Gateway:

- Strong authentication methods such as smartcards, one-time password, and token authentication are enabled.
- Pre-authentication that requires users to log on to the UAG server before gaining access to the RD Gateway is enabled.
- Single sign on allows credentials used for session logon to be used for access to RDS hosts and RemoteApps.
- Endpoint detection via Network Access Protection (NAP) determines a remote client's health before the client is allowed to access Remote Desktop Services resources.
- A single point of access enables you to focus on Forefront UAG for monitoring and reporting for RD Gateway connections.
- Array and high availability for the RD Gateway solution ensure that users can always connect when they need to connect to RDS-hosted resources.

Remote Desktop Gateway publishing is another key scenario enabled by UAG and should be the preferred solution for any enterprise RD Gateway deployment.

Remote Access Client VPN Services

IAG included a feature called the Network Connector that allowed users to connect to the corporate network over a network-level SSL VPN connection. Though the Network Connector did provide the ability to create a network-level VPN connection over SSL, which was very useful for users located behind firewalls or Web proxies that didn't allow other outbound VPN protocols, it was somewhat limited, because little access control could be performed over the Network Connection session, and there was no application layer inspection performed over the Network Connector established links.

UAG improves this situation by including support for SSTP. SSTP allows users who are located behind restrictive firewalls and Web proxy devices to connect over an HTTPS connection to the UAG SSTP remote access VPN server. Additionally, because UAG leverages TMG to enable SSTP, you can take advantage of the strong user, group, and destination access control in TMG to help enforce a "least privilege" approach to remote access VPN client connections.

Other New Features

Forefront UAG includes a host of other new features that will be of interest to any remote access gateway administrator. These include:

- NAP support for endpoint detection

- Endpoint detection for non-Microsoft browsers and operating systems
- A new portal appearance with an Outlook Web Access and Outlook Web App look and feel
- Comprehensive support for Kerberos Constrained Delegation and Active Directory Federation Services (AD FS)
- Logging to SQL server
- An Activation Monitor that enables tracking of configuration activity

Table 1-2 provides information about other differences between IAG and UAG.

TABLE 1-2 Forefront IAG and UAG IAG feature comparison

FEATURE	SUPPORTED IN UAG	SUPPORTED IN IAG SP2	DETAILS
ActivePerl installation	No	Yes	ActivePerl is not required in Forefront UAG.
Multi-server deployment	Yes	No	IAG did not support multi-server arrays.
SSTP VPN	Yes	No	IAG did not support SSTP remote access VPN client connections.
Publishing Exchange services with dedicated wizard	Yes	No	UAG includes a dedicated wizard to publish OWA, ActiveSync, and RPC/HTTP in a single portal, using a single IP address for all three services.
Publishing Exchange 2003 Outlook Mobile Access	No	Yes	Support for OMA was dropped in UAG.
Publishing Remote Desktop Gateway	Yes	No	IAG did not support publishing desktop services gateway.
Windows Integrated Authentication	No	Yes	Support for Windows Integrated Authentication was dropped in UAG.
Web farm load balancing	Yes	No	UAG enables publishing of Web Farms using Web Farm Load Balancing, eliminating the need for NLB or expensive external load balancers.
Endpoint detection via NAP	Yes	No	IAG did not support NAP endpoint detection.
Activation Monitor	Yes	No	IAG did not include an Activation Monitor.
Policy Manager	No	Yes	Policy manager was dropped in UAG.

Session Manager	No	Yes	Session manager was dropped in UAG.
Web mail trunk	No	Yes	Web mail trunk was dropped in UAG.
Basic trunk	No	Yes	Basic trunk was dropped in UAG.
Application templates dropped in UAG	N/A	N/A	▓ FTP (Passive Mode) ▓ iSeries Access for Windows (VSR3) ▓ Telnet Microsoft ▓ Windows 2000 Terminal Services Client ▓ Domino Offline Service; Domino Offline Services 7.0 ▓ Outlook (Internet Mail Only Mode) ▓ Outlook Express 5.x and Outlook Express 6.x ▓ Windows Mail ▓ Native Notes Client (Multi-Servers); Native Notes Client (Single Server) ▓ Logon Server ▓ Sametime Native (Chat Only); Sametime Native Relay (Chat Only) ▓ Generic Mac OS X Carbon App (hosts required/optional/disabled)
Publishing browser-enable application templates dropped in UAG	N/A	N/A	▓ Generic Browser-Embedded app ▓ Domino iNotes (single/multiple) ▓ Citrix NFuse FR3 (Direct) ▓ Citrix Presentation Server (Web Interface 3.0/4.0/4/5) ▓ Citrix Secure Access Manger (Direct/Via Secure Gateway) ▓ Sametime Native/Plug-in ▓ IBM Host-On-Demand 8.0 ▓ Terminal Services Web Client (Single Server) ▓ NetManage Rumba Web-to-Host 4.2

Publishing Web application templates dropped	N/A	N/A	▪ Exchange 2000 Server
			▪ Lotus Domino iNotes 8.0
			▪ Lotus Domino Web Mail (4.x,5.x,6.x,7.x)
			▪ Microsoft CRM 3.0
			▪ PeopleSoft 8.9
			▪ WebSphere Portal 5.02
			▪ SAP Enterprise Portal 6.0

When to Use Forefront UAG

It can be confusing to decide when to use Forefront UAG and when to use Forefront TMG. The decision about whether to use one product or the other should be based on the scenario and on your needs. Forefront UAG is the primary Microsoft offering for enterprise-level application publishing and SSL VPN solutions. This release of Forefront UAG offers enough capabilities to make it a centralized access gateway for today's complex, large, and distributed enterprise networks. Although Forefront TMG has publishing capabilities (like its predecessor ISA Server 2006 had), the level of customization and flexibility that Forefront UAG offers is both more robust and granular and goes well beyond the capabilities of Forefront TMG.

> **NOTE** You can view a table that compares ISA and UAG in "Secure Application Access," at *http://www.microsoft.com/forefront/edgesecurity/en/us/secure-application-access.aspx*. This will give you some ideas about how to decide between them.

When planning a Forefront UAG deployment, consider whether any of the following options is necessary to meet your company's requirements:

- Allow anywhere access to internal applications through a single portal and perform endpoint compliance scans.
- Enable integration with Windows Server 2008 R2 DirectAccess.
- Enable users to access internal applications using SSTP.
- Allow integration with NAP and endpoint scans while accessing the main portal.
- Customize the main portal and the authentication method.

If you need at least one of these features, Forefront UAG is the right choice for you. Next, you should evaluate the needs of your organization, the scenario in which you are going to use Forefront UAG, and the expectations for this access gateway.

Another important consideration when you are deciding whether to use Forefront UAG or Forefront TMG is your requirement for outbound access control. Forefront UAG is a remote-access-only solution and is used only for inbound access control. In contrast, Forefront TMG enables both inbound and outbound access control, Web anti-malware for outbound access, and Network Inspection Service for strong IDS/IPS capabilities. Most enterprise deployments of Forefront TMG separate inbound and outbound duties, so enterprise arrays are dedicated to inbound or outbound access; however, for mid-sized and small businesses, you might decide, for cost reasons, to use Forefront TMG and consolidate inbound and outbound access controls to a single server or an array of servers.

If you do not need an outbound access control solution, or if you already have Forefront TMG in place for outbound access control, the question is whether you should use Forefront TMG or Forefront UAG for inbound access control. Forefront UAG has the following advantages for inbound access control:

- Forefront UAG supports a wider array of authentication protocols.
- Forefront UAG supports an integrated and enterprise-ready DirectAccess solution.
- Forefront UAG provides more sophisticated application layer inspection for incoming Web connections.
- Forefront UAG includes integrated support for hosting, managing, and monitoring a Remote Desktop Services Gateway.

In general, the best recommendation is that if your budget supports purchasing Forefront UAG as your Remote Access Gateway solution, Forefront UAG is the best solution for your organization. However, if your budget does not support a Forefront UAG purchase, Forefront TMG is a good choice.

Administrator's Punch List

In this chapter, you learned about key features and capabilities included with Forefront Unified Access Gateway 2010. The following list includes concepts that are important to remember:

- Forefront UAG is a 64-bit-only application.
- Forefront UAG must be installed on Windows Server 2008 R2 or above.
- Forefront UAG supports SSTP as its only remote access VPN protocol.
- Forefront UAG supports DirectAccess, a new seamless remote access solution for Windows 7 clients.

- Forefront UAG can host the Remote Desktop Gateway Server role.
- Forefront TMG is installed on the Forefront UAG server to protect the network behind the UAG server, as well as to protect the Forefront UAG server itself.
- Forefront UAG supports an array configuration in which all servers in a Forefront UAG array represent a single logical Forefront UAG server.
- Forefront UAG supports Network Load Balancer to provide high availability and connection balancing.
- Forefront UAG provides a portal page, so users can access Web resources over a reverse-proxy connection.
- Forefront UAG includes the Network Connector, a legacy network-level SSL VPN connection to the corporate network. SSTP is the preferred network-level SSL VPN connection method.
- Forefront UAG supports NAP for endpoint protection.
- Forefront UAG includes a built-in endpoint protection feature that can be used for non-NAP capable clients.

CHAPTER 2

Planning and Installing Forefront UAG

▪ Planning Forefront UAG Deployment   **15**

▪ Hardware Requirements   **26**

▪ Software Requirements   **26**

▪ Installing Forefront UAG   **29**

▪ Configuring Forefront UAG   **34**

▪ Deploying a Forefront UAG Array   **43**

Proper planning helps ensure that your deployment is able to meet your design goals, and proper deployment helps make it possible for your plans to come to life. This chapter discusses the way to plan your UAG deployment. It also includes a discussion about key network, infrastructure, and software requirements that enable the installation and deployment scenarios. The chapter ends with details about the way to install UAG in stand-alone and array configurations.

Planning Forefront UAG Deployment

When planning a Microsoft Forefront Unified Access Gateway (UAG) 2010 deployment, it's important to keep in mind that the Forefront UAG server or array acts not only as a network device, but also as a network server in a client/server role. You need to take into account a number of network services that are required to meet your deployment needs. These include:

- Corporate Access Model
- Name Resolution
- Public Key Infrastructure
- Domain and Workgroup Membership
- IPv6 Considerations
- External and Internal Firewalls

- Fault Tolerance and Load Balancing
- Network Access Protection

This section will go into more detail about each of these important network and network services components of a Forefront UAG solution.

Corporate Access Model

The first item you must consider when planning your Forefront UAG deployment is the access model you intend to use for your remote users. The Forefront UAG server is designed to meet the needs of several different populations of users. The primary access models for Forefront UAG remote access users include:

- **Reverse proxy or portal**   The reverse proxy or portal access model allows you to provide least-privilege access to users who are internal or external to your organization. This access model is ideal if you want to limit access to a select group of applications for a particular user or group. The downside of this model is that user access is limited to Web applications.

- **Port or socket forwarding**   The port or socket forwarding access model allows users to access non-Web-based server applications. This provides the user with a more robust end-user experience, but, like the reverse proxy model, this model limits access to select applications and does not enable the richest end-user experience.

- **Network-level SSL VPN**   The network-level SSL VPN access model uses either the SSTP or Network Connector features included with Forefront UAG. The Network Connector is a lightweight application that is downloaded by the remote client. After the Network Connector is installed, users create a network-level SSL VPN connection to the corporate network. Network Connector is for computers running either Windows operating systems that are earlier than Vista SP1 or non-Windows operating systems. For Windows PCs running Vista SP1 and above, SSTP is the preferred network-level VPN connection. This access model should be reserved for administrators and other highly trusted users only, because it provides complete network access from computers that are not known to be highly managed or secured.

- **DirectAccess**   DirectAccess is a new remote access technology enabled by Windows Server 2008 R2 and Windows 7. Although you can run DirectAccess using only Windows Server 2008 R2 as the DirectAccess server, Forefront UAG enables enterprise functionality and availability to the DirectAccess solution. DirectAccess provides a true "on network" experience for DirectAccess clients for both the end user and IT.

Forefront UAG supports mixed access models, which means you can deploy multiple access models on a single machine. For example, if you want to run DirectAccess and SSTP remote access services on the same Forefront UAG server or array, you can do that. It is also possible to deploy all access models on the same Forefront UAG server or array. By serving multiple access models, Forefront UAG enables you to have a *unified* remote access solution, in which configuration, monitoring, and reporting are done from a single location.

Name Resolution

Name resolution is critical in two main areas:

- Internet name resolution
- Intranet name resolution

Internet Name Resolution

Internet name resolution is important because remote users need to be able to resolve the name or names of the Forefront UAG server's external IP address or addresses. Your public DNS server needs to include Host (A) records for the names of the trunks you want to create when publishing Web sites and portals. If you have sites or portals, each of those names needs to be resolvable to the IP address that you have bound to the site or portal.

Internet name resolution is also important when setting up Forefront UAG as a remote access VPN server. However, there is an additional consideration when using SSTP: The remote access VPN client needs to be able to resolve the name of the Certificate Revocation Server (CRL) listed on the server certificate delivered to the client by the Forefront UAG server. If the SSTP client cannot access the CRL, the SSTP connection will fail. However, it is a best practice to use a commercial certificate for your SSTP listener. In that case, the CRL is globally available and you don't have to worry about your remote access clients being able to reach the CRL.

In a similar vein, DirectAccess clients need to be able to resolve the name of the IP-HTTPS listener to connect to the Forefront UAG DirectAccess server when 6to4 or Teredo are not available. (IP-HTTPS is an IPv6 transition protocol that allows DirectAccess clients to connect to the DirectAccess server over an IPv4 Internet, and Teredo is another IPv6 transition technology.) In addition, the DirectAccess client needs to be able to connect to the CRL listed on the IP-HTTPS server certificate, so it must be able to resolve the name of the Web server that is hosting the CRL. As with the SSTP listener, it is a best practice to use a commercial Certificate Authority (CA) for the IP-HTTPS certificate. This will make the CRL globally available.

Internal Name Resolution

Internal name resolution is critical in for a number of reasons:

- The Forefront UAG server needs to be able to resolve the names of the published servers.
- The Forefront UAG server needs to be able to resolve the names of the authentication repositories.
- The Forefront UAG server needs to be able to resolve the names of domain controllers.
- Clients on the internal network need to resolve the name Intra-Site Automatic Tunnel Addressing Protocol (ISATAP) to the internal IP address of the Forefront UAG

server, because the Forefront UAG server acts as an ISATAP router in a DirectAccess deployment.

- Clients on the internal network need to be able to resolve the names of the Network Location Servers in a DirectAccess deployment.

- Clients on the internal network need to be able to resolve the names of the servers on the internal network that is hosting the CRL for certificates used on the network location servers.

The DirectAccess name resolution requirements are critical because if the DirectAccess client on the corporate network is unable to contact the network location server, the DirectAccess client will understand that failure to mean that it is on the Internet, and it will try to act as a DirectAccess client on the corporate network. This will cause a failure of communications while the DirectAccess is connected to the corporate network. In addition, the DirectAccess client must be able resolve the name of the server hosting the CRL listed on the network location server's certificate and connect to that server to retrieve the CRL. If the CRL is not available, the connection to the network location server will fail, and the DirectAccess client will not know that it is on the corporate network.

Public Key Infrastructure

Forefront UAG takes advantage of a Public Key Infrastructure (PKI) and certificates in a number of ways. These include:

- **Web site certificates**   Web site certificates are used in a number of places, such as the IP-HTTPS listener used by DirectAccess clients, Web portals, SSTP VPN listeners, and network location servers. Web site certificates can be from public or private Certificate Authorities, depending on the scenario. Commercial (public) certificates are best used on listeners that accept connections from Internet-based clients, while private certificates are the most effective solution for clients that connect from the corporate network.

- **CA certificates**   CA certificates are required on all machines that need to trust the certificates being delivered to them. These can be public or private Certificate Authorities.

- **Computer certificates**   Computer certificates are assigned to DirectAccess clients and DirectAccess servers to support IPsec tunnel establishment between the DirectAccess clients and servers. In addition, application servers can use computer certificates to support transport mode IPsec connections between DirectAccess clients and the application servers.

When planning your Forefront UAG deployment, consider the locations in which you are going to use public certificates and those in which you are going to use private certificates. Most enterprise deployments already have a well-defined PKI, and Forefront UAG can take advantage of your current PKI to obtain Web site and computer certificates. However, if your organization does not currently have a PKI in place, let the Forefront UAG implementation be motivation for starting one. Windows Server 2003 SP2 and above can support all the internal certificate requirements for your Forefront UAG installation. When installing the Microsoft Certificate Services, make sure that you create an enterprise CA, so that the CA certificates are automatically deployed to all domain members. If there are servers in your design that are not domain members, you will need to export the CA certificate and then import it into the Trusted Root Certification Authorities machine certificate store on the non-domain members.

Domain and Workgroup Membership

Forefront UAG can be deployed as either a domain member or a workgroup member. The domain membership requirements are based on the access and authentication models you choose. The following are important scenarios to consider before you decide whether or not to make the Forefront UAG server a domain or workgroup member:

- You require users to connect to the corporate network over a network level SSTP connection. If so, this requires that the Forefront UAG server must be a domain member. (Note: This is the Forefront UAG RTM behavior by design.)

- You require single sign on with Kerberos Constrained Delegation (KCD). KCD allows users and computers to present certificates to the Forefront UAG server for authentication. The certificate-based credentials can then be converted and forwarded to application servers as Kerberos credentials. This enables single sign on because the Forefront UAG server can accept the certificate-based credentials from the client and then forward them, on-demand, as Kerberos credentials, when the Web server asks for them. KCD requires that the Forefront UAG server be a domain member.

- You require that Forefront UAG provide file server access. One of Forefront UAG's key roles as an SSL VPN server is to provide an Explorer-like file access experience within the browser interface. This has been a popular access scenario for IAG, and it is likely to continue to be popular with Forefront UAG. If you want to provide this file server access feature to your users, the Forefront UAG server will need to be a domain member.

- You require that the Forefront UAG deployment be fault-tolerant and highly available. The Forefront UAG server plays a central role in your remote access plan. If the Forefront UAG deployment fails for any reason, all your remote access users will be disconnected from corporate resources, making fault tolerance and high availability mandatory in any enterprise deployment. The Forefront UAG server array must be joined to the domain in order to support array creation and configuration.

- You require DirectAccess connectivity. While DirectAccess is available with both Windows Server 2008 R2 Standard and Windows Server 2008 R2 Enterprise editions, the Windows DirectAccess feature set doesn't meet the high availability and fault tolerance requirements of most enterprises. If you need your Forefront UAG array to act as a DirectAccess server array, it will need to be joined to the domain.

Admin Insight: Why Choose Domain Deployment?

I n general, domain deployment is the superior option because it enables the entire set of security and access features that are available in Forefront UAG. Whether there are any security advantages gained by not joining the Forefront UAG server or array to the domain is debatable. (And, of course, most enterprise environments contain multiple domains and forests.) While, in many network security groups, there is historical concern over Internet-facing domain members, this concern is mostly based on issues with Windows NT SMB and legacy Web services. Windows Server 2008 R2 bears little relation to the security models used in those areas. While there are no guarantees, the Microsoft Forefront UAG Product Team is confident that you can place the Forefront UAG server or array in a domain without concern about creating a larger attack surface.

IPv6 Considerations

When Forefront UAG is deployed as a reverse Web proxy or portal server, a port or socket-forwarding server, or an SSTP or Network Connector network-level VPN server, only IPv4 is supported. If you have IPv6-only applications, or want to connect from the IPv6 Internet, you will not be able to connect to the Forefront UAG server. The only IPv6-aware connection model is the DirectAccess server deployment. Note that DirectAccess server deployment does not exclude the other corporate connectivity models; you can co-locate all models with the DirectAccess corporate connection model.

IPv6 is the foundation of DirectAccess connectivity. The details of DirectAccess and IPv6 issues included with a DirectAccess deployment are the topic of Chapter 5, "Implementing Forefront UAG with DirectAccess." However, if you want to support a DirectAccess client connection to the corporate network, you will want to consider your current IPv6-readiness and your plans for IPv6 in the future during your planning.

You should not consider lack of IPv6-readiness as a block to Forefront UAG DirectAccess, because Forefront UAG includes technologies that allow DirectAccess clients to connect to an IPv4-only intranet. These technologies are NAT64 and DNS64. The NAT64 feature enables the Forefront UAG server to translate IPv6 communications from the DirectAccess client to IPv4-only resources on the corporate network. The DNS64 feature enables the Forefront UAG server to "spoof" an IPv6 address to deliver to the DirectAccess client, so that it can connect to an IPv4-only resource. With NAT64/DNS64, Forefront UAG needs to be the only IPv6-aware server on your network. You can even have Windows Server 2003 domain controllers, and Forefront UAG DirectAccess will enable full network connectivity for DirectAccess clients.

However, to fully realize the benefits of Forefront UAG DirectAccess, you should consider upgrading your infrastructure servers and management servers to an IPv6-aware operating system, such as Windows Server 2008 or above. It's important to understand that being

IPv6-aware is not the same as being IPv6-native. In an IPv6-native network, the entire routing, operating system, application, and management infrastructure is configured to support IPv6, and native IPv6 addresses are used throughout the network. In contrast, an IPv6-aware network is one that can use IPv6 and support IPv6 applications, but typically represents a mixture of IPv4 and IPv6 resources.

Since there are few IPv6-native networks, you do not need to understand the intricacies of IPv6 IP addressing, routing, and supporting services to deploy Forefront UAG DirectAccess. However, you will benefit most from the Forefront UAG DirectAccess solution by using IPv6-aware hosts on the corporate network that support the ISATAP. ISATAP will configure your IPv6-aware resources with a native IPv6 address so that IPv6 services can communicate with each other. However, ISATAP allows you to encapsulate the IPv6 packets with an IPv4 header, so that they can be routed over your current IPv4 routing infrastructure. When the ISATAP IPv4 encapsulated packet reaches its destination, the IPv4 header is removed to expose the IPv6 packet, which is delivered to the application.

For planning purposes, you will want to assess your current IPv6-readiness. If you have no IPv6-aware servers, Forefront UAG DirectAccess will still work, but you will not be able to take advantage of the "manage out" features that are available when you have IPv6-aware management servers on your network. You will also want to consider any plans you have for migrating to an IPv6-only network in the future. If you will be moving to an IPv6-only network, you'll need to work with your network people to develop a plan to migrate from ISATAP to native IPv6. However, native IPv6 networks are likely a decade or more away. The only things that might change this are government mandates for IPv6-native networking or a "must have" application that depends on them. Neither of these events seems likely.

External and Internal Firewalls

There is some debate about whether a firewall should be placed in front of the Forefront UAG server. On one hand, the TMG firewall is co-located on the Forefront UAG server, so there is built-in firewall protection. However, the Forefront UAG Support Boundaries statement says that the TMG is intended to support only the Forefront UAG server host computer and should not be used as a network firewall. This is a somewhat vague statement; it doesn't explain whether this supportability limitation is due to the fact that Forefront UAG is for inbound access only, and would thus be of little use as a network firewall, or whether there are some security issues with the services running the Forefront UAG component that prevent it from effectively blocking attacks from the outside.

Admin Insight: Using a Perimeter Network

The subject of whether or not to use a perimeter network has been debated quite a bit, and the consensus is that if you have an established perimeter network (also known as a demilitarized zone or DMZ), as most enterprises already do, there is no reason not to take advantage of your current deployment, and therefore place the Forefront UAG server or array in the perimeter network. However, if you're a small or midsized business, there is no reason to create a new perimeter network just to support the Forefront UAG server; the TMG components are there to protect you from external attack. However, this Forefront UAG deployment will need to be parallel to your current firewall implementation, since the Forefront UAG server can't be used for outbound access.

Another viable option is to create a back-to-back configuration with the Forefront UAG located behind a front-end firewall, with a perimeter network between the firewall and the external interface of the Forefront UAG server or array. This will not create problems for the SSL VPN reverse proxy clients. However, there will be routing issues if you choose to use the Forefront UAG server as a VPN server, because they will not be using the Forefront UAG server as an IPv4 default gateway. However, these issues are not uncommon, and there are standard fixes for them. The DirectAccess scenario is unaffected, because ISATAP will configure the Forefront UAG server to be the ISATAP router for the network.

Admin Insight: Back-End Firewall Required?

As for a back-end firewall, there is no reason at all to provide a back-end firewall to support only the Forefront UAG server or array. However, if you already have a perimeter network configured that has both front-end and back-end firewalls encasing the perimeter, there's no reason not to take advantage of your established deployment. This will make firewall configuration and management more difficult and more liable for error, which could introduce a point of failure in your security design. But if it is your corporate policy to have an internal firewall, you will have to do your best to avoid security issues introduced by such a complex firewall policy. However, if you do not already have an internal firewall, we do not recommend that you deploy one just to support the Forefront UAG server or array.

Table 2-1 provides information regarding the protocols that need to be enabled on the front-end firewall, and Table 2-2 lists the protocols that need to be enabled on the back-end firewall.

TABLE 2-1 External firewall settings

PROTOCOL	DESTINATION
HTTP inbound (TCP port 80)	External IP address on UAG HTTP listener
HTTPS inbound (TCP port 443)	External IP address on UAG SSL listener

TABLE 2-2 Internal firewall settings

PROTOCOL	DESTINATION
Microsoft-DS traffic TCP 445 UDP 445	Domain controllers
Kerberos authentication TCP 88 UDP 88	Domain controllers
LDAP TCP 389 UDP 389	Domain controllers
LDAPS TCP 636 UDP 636	Domain controllers
LDAP to GC TCP 3268 UDP 3268	Domain controllers
LDAPS to GC TCP 3269 UDP 3269	Domain controllers
DNS UDP 53 TCP 53	DNS servers
RADIUS UDP 1645 Or UDP 1812	RADIUS servers
SecureID ACE UDP 5500	SecureID ACE servers

NOTE Tables 2-1 and 2-2 do not include the protocols to use when the Forefront UAG server is also acting as a DirectAccess server.

When the Forefront UAG server also acts as a DirectAccess server, on the external firewall you will need to allow UDP port 3544 inbound and outbound and TCP protocol 41 inbound and outbound. If the Forefront UAG DirectAccess server is on the IPv6 Internet, you will need to allow IP protocol 50, UDP port 500 inbound and outbound, and all ICMPv6 traffic inbound and outbound.

If you have an internal firewall behind the Forefront UAG DirectAccess server, you will need to allow all IPv4 TCP and UDP traffic inbound and outbound, all IPv6 traffic inbound and outbound, and all ICMPv6 traffic inbound and outbound between the Forefront UAG DirectAccess server and the entire intranet.

Fault Tolerance and Load Balancing

When planning for fault tolerance and load balancing, you will need to consider how to best accomplish each. For fault tolerance, Forefront UAG enables you to configure arrays of Forefront UAG servers. A Forefront UAG server array is configured as, and acts like, a single logical Forefront UAG server. Configuration is performed once, at the array manager, and then is distributed automatically to all the array members. When one member of the array fails, it is possible for other array members to take over for the failing member.

In order to accomplish fault tolerance for the array, you need a method of load balancing that will automatically remove the failed array member from the network so that it no longer services connections. This can be accomplished by using integrated Network Load Balancing (NLB). Forefront UAG is integrated with Network Load Balancing so that configuration is performed in the Forefront UAG console rather than in the Windows Network Load Balancing console. Do not configure NLB on the Forefront UAG server in the Windows Network Load Balancing console, or your settings will be overwritten by the Forefront UAG configuration.

Forefront UAG supports multicast, unicast, and Internet Group Management Protocol (IGMP) multicast modes. However, if you need to make the Forefront UAG server a DirectAccess server, you must choose unicast mode. DirectAccess does not support multicast or IGMP multicast modes.

Another option for load balancing a fault-tolerant Forefront UAG array is to configure it to use an external load balancer. While an external load balancer can provide some performance advantages over NLB (because NLB is limited to approximately 500 Mbps), the external load balancer becomes an additional point of failure, and you will need to deploy at least two load balancers to provide fault tolerance and failover for the external load balancers. In addition, if you are deploying DirectAccess on your Forefront UAG array, you will need to acquire a load balancer that is compatible with Forefront UAG DirectAccess. At the time of this writing, F5 was the only company that had announced that it was building a load balancer with DirectAccess support.

Network Access Protection

One of the key features included with Forefront UAG is endpoint detection. Forefront UAG enables access that is based not only on the user who logs into the portal, but also on the machine that connects to the portal. You might have a highly trusted user, but if that user is connecting from a machine with low security, you do not want to allow that user privileged access. In fact, you would want to downgrade that user's rights and limit the options that are available, even for applications to which the user already has rights.

Forefront UAG provides two methods for performing endpoint detection to determine whether the computer from which a user is attempting access is safe. You can use the built-in endpoint detection feature, or you can use Microsoft Network Access Protection. The built-in endpoint detection is much more robust in its ability to make assessments regarding the endpoint than the NAP detection mechanism is, due to the small number of checks that are enabled by the default Windows System Health Validator (SHV). However, if you have created your SHVs or have incorporated vendor SHVs that provide high value to your organization, you might find that your NAP detection capabilities are far superior to what is available from the Forefront UAG endpoint detection feature. (The small number of checks available in the Windows SHV made NAP less successful in the market than it should have been.) Although Forefront UAG endpoint detection and access policies are relatively easy to configure, if you choose NAP you will need to build out a new NAP infrastructure or use an existing one. If you do not have a current NAP infrastructure, you will need to:

- Install a Network Policy Server (NPS).
- Configure the Forefront UAG server as an NPS client.
- Configure NAP health policies.
- Configure NAP network policies.
- Define the NPS server in the Forefront UAG console.
- Enable NAP on the trunk you created for the published site.

It is important to note that you can use the integrated endpoint detection feature included with Forefront UAG only for sites and portals that use trunks. You cannot enable NAP for network layer SSTP VPN connections. This is in contrast to Microsoft Forefront Threat Management Gateway (TMG) 2010, in which NAP access control is possible.

You should consider NAP a critical component of your overall security architecture for DirectAccess clients. If you plan to configure the Forefront UAG server as a DirectAccess server, NAP enforcement should be high on your list of protection mechanisms. Remember, the DirectAccess client is always away from the office, but it also always connected to the office. This means that the DirectAccess client should be as highly managed as those clients that reside in the corporate office. In addition to using Group Policy or Configuration Manager to maintain the required security configuration for the DirectAccess clients (and the rest of your network), you will want to make sure that all patches are installed and that the anti-malware system on the DirectAccess client is also on and fully up to date. NAP will take advantage of your underlying security management infrastructure and confirm that many of its components are instantiated on the DirectAccess client before enabling that client's network access.

Hardware Requirements

There are hardware and software requirements you need to address before deploying Forefront UAG on your network. Hardware requirements include:

- A dual core processor running at 2.66 GHz or above.
- At least 4 GB of system memory (RAM).
- Two network adapters. Although it is possible to get a single network adapter configuration running, the installer will not allow this.
- At least 2.5 GB of disk space available for the Forefront UAG software installation.

Software Requirements

Before you begin installing the Forefront UAG server or array, you need to understand the software requirements for:

- Forefront UAG servers
- Forefront UAG clients

Forefront UAG Server Software Requirements

Software requirements for Forefront UAG servers include:

- Windows Server 2008 R2 Standard or Enterprise Edition. Forefront UAG will not install on Windows Server 2008.
- Remote installations of Forefront UAG can be performed over RDP. However, the installation files must be local on both local and remote installations. You cannot install UAG from installation files on a remote file share.
- If you choose remote installation over RDP, the connection must be over IPv4, because Forefront UAG does not support IPv6 connections for Forefront UAG software installation.
- Forefront UAG server software should be installed on a clean operating system. No other network servers or service should be installed on the Forefront UAG server. An exception to this is host antivirus software. Ideally, antivirus software should be installed after Forefront UAG is installed, and then all Forefront UAG directories should be excluded from scanning.
- The Forefront UAG installer will install the Forefront TMG management console. However, all configuration will be done within the Forefront UAG management console. It is highly recommended that you do not perform any configuration within the Forefront TMG console, outside of those configurations described in the support boundaries document for Forefront UAG.

- You must be a domain user and a local administrator on the Forefront UAG computer to install Forefront UAG. You do not need domain administrator permissions to install Forefront UAG.

- If the Forefront UAG server or array is configured as a workgroup, configure the server or the array servers with the appropriate DNS suffixes so that single label names are fully qualified before they are sent to internal DNS servers.

- If you are running Forefront UAG on Microsoft Hyper-V, the host operating system must run Windows Server 2008 SP2 or Windows Server 2008 R2.

Admin Insight: Avoiding problems

It is recommended that you always have the Internal network interface card on the top of the binding order. Not having this in place can cause issues such as the one documented at *http://blogs.technet.com/b/yuridiogenes/archive/2010/08/16 /unable-to-install-forefront-tmg-2010-error-0x80074e46.aspx*.

Forefront UAG Client Requirements

Forefront UAG client requirements are a bit more complex because of the number of possible client/server interactions you can see, depending on the type of connectivity required by the client. Table 2-3 provides some details on client requirements and capabilities.

TABLE 2-3 Forefront UAG client requirements and support

OPERATING SYSTEM	SUPPORTED BROWSERS	CLIENT COMPONENT
32-bit operating systems: - Windows XP with SP2 or SP3 - Windows Vista RTM with SP1 - Windows 7	IE6, IE7, and IE8 Firefox 3.0.x Firefox 3.5.x Safari 3.2.x Safari 4.0.x	The following are supported on Windows operating systems that are running supported browsers: - Endpoint session cleanup - Endpoint detection - SSL application tunneling - Socket forwarding - Endpoint quarantine enforcement - Remote Desktop Services The following components are supported only on select operating systems: - Windows XP: Network Connector - Windows Vista: Network Connector - Windows 7: SSTP and DirectAccess

64-bit operating systems: ■ Windows Vista RTM with SP1 ■ Windows 7 ■ Windows Server 2008 R2	Only 32-bit browsers are supported: IE6, IE7, and IE8 Firefox 3.0.x Firefox 3.5.x Safari 3.2.x Safari 4.0.x	Client components that can run on Windows operating systems with supported browsers: ■ Endpoint Session Cleanup ■ Endpoint detection (Endpoint detection does not work on Windows Server 2008 R2) ■ SSTP ■ Endpoint Quarantine Enforcement ■ Remote Desktop Services Components that work only on select operating systems: ■ Vista: Network Connector ■ Windows 7: DirectAccess
Mac OS X 10.4 and up (PowerPC and Intel)	Firefox 3.0.x Firefox 3.5.x Safari 3.2.x Safari 4.0.x	Java client components are used with Safari and Firefox. The client components that are supported: ■ Endpoint Session Cleanup ■ Endpoint detection ■ SSL application tunneling
Linux 32-bit operating systems (RPM-based distributions): ■ Red Hat Enterprise 5 ■ Fedora 10 and up ■ Debian Linux distributions ■ Debian 5 and up ■ Ubuntu 8.04 LTS and 9.04 and up	Firefox 3.0.x Firefox 3.5.x	Java components supported with Firefox: ■ Endpoint Session Cleanup ■ Endpoint detection ■ SSL application tunneling
Windows Mobile 2005 Windows Mobile 6 Windows Mobile 6.5	Pocket Internet Explorer Windows Mobile 6.5 supports the premium mobile portal	
iPhone version 3.0.x	Safari (iPhone version), supports the premium mobile portal	

Nokia:	All handsets support the limited mobile portal
▪ S60 3rd edition, Feature Pack 1 – validated on E71, N95	
▪ S60 3rd edition, Feature Pack 2 – validated on E72, E52	
▪ S60 5th edition – validated on N97	

Other Forefront UAG client issues of which you should be aware include:

- Windows operating systems need to support ActiveX controls. The browser must be configured to support the downloading and running of signed ActiveX objects.
- Other browsers might work with Forefront UAG, but they have not been tested, so there are no guarantees of full functionality.
- Local administrator privileges are required to install the Java Endpoint Detection and Endpoint Session Cleanup applets.
- There is no offline installation option for Java components; the client must be connected to the portal.
- The Java Runtime Environment (JRE) 1.5 or above is required.
- Administrator privileges are required to install the ActiveX components.

Installing Forefront UAG

Once you finish planning your Forefront UAG deployment and have met all the hardware and software requirements, you will be almost ready to install. You also should add the IP address of each network interface on Windows prior to starting the Forefront UAG installation. One final recommendation: Make sure that you run Windows Update before starting the installation to make sure Windows is up to date. This is a very important step to ensure that Forefront UAG will be installed on the latest version of Windows Server 2008. Internally, the installation process uses the following logic:

- Stage 1: Setup performs pre-prerequisite checks.
- Stage 2: Setup automatically installs prerequisite software:
  - AJAX toolkit
  - Operating system roles and features
  - Forefront TMG

- Stage 3: Setup runs msiexec.exe with ForefrontUAG.msi as input.
  - In attended mode, if any of the components require restart, the setup notifies the user.
  - In unattended mode, the setup process automatically restarts unless you specifically indicate that it should not.

NOTE **Forefront UAG setup logs are stored at %ProgramData%\Microsoft\UAG\Logs.**

At each stage of the setup process, the return codes are checked. If any installation fails, Setup rolls back the installation, but roles and features are not rolled back. Now that you know what to expect from the setup process, you are ready to start the installation. Put the Forefront UAG DVD on the server's DVD drive, and follow these steps:

1. Windows should read the DVD content and start the installation based on the autorun parameters. When this happens you will see a splash screen similar to that shown in Figure 2-1. (If autorun is disabled, then open and execute the file splash.hta, and the same splash screen should appear.)

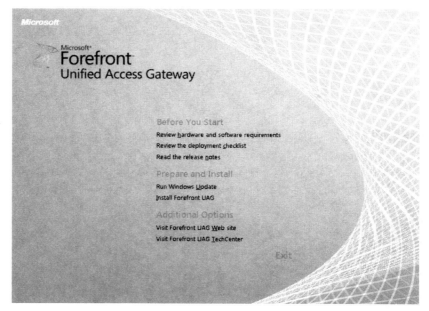

FIGURE 2-1

2. As you can see in Figure 2-1, you have a chance to perform a last review of the hardware and software components, as well as to run Windows Update. Assuming that all those components are correct or complete and you have all the latest software

updates installed, click Install Forefront UAG. If you have less than 4 GB on your server, the message shown in Figure 2-2 will appear.

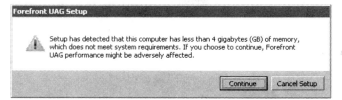

FIGURE 2-2

3. It is very important to understand that this warning serves to remind you not only that you have less than 4 GB, but also that the real message behind this is that the overall Forefront UAG performance will be affected because the operating system doesn't have the appropriate hardware size. If you are installing Forefront UAG in a lab environment for testing purposes, even if you see the warning, you can safely click Continue to proceed. Figure 2-3 shows the first page of the Forefront UAG Setup Wizard.

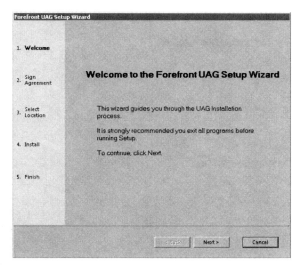

FIGURE 2-3

4. Click Next in the first screen to proceed and the Sign Agreement page shown in Figure 2-4 appears.

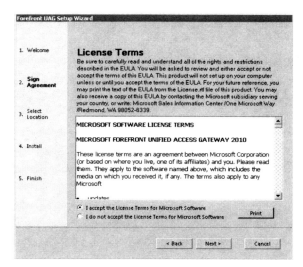

FIGURE 2-4

5. Read the License Terms and then select I Accept The License Terms For Microsoft Software. Click Next to continue, and the page shown in Figure 2-5 appears.

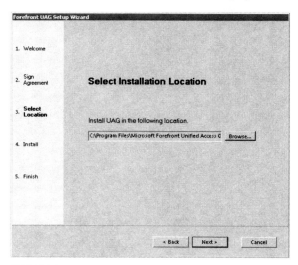

FIGURE 2-5

6. On this screen you should choose the Forefront UAG installation location based on the deployment planning you have done. If, during the planning phase, you decided to install Forefront UAG on a separate disk from the operating system, this is your chance to do this. For the purposes of this walkthrough, leave the default option selected. Click Next to continue, and the page shown in Figure 2-6 appears.

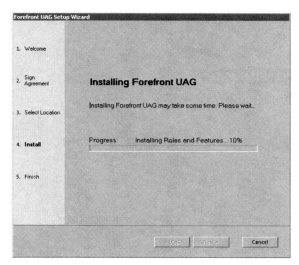

FIGURE 2-6

7. At this point Forefront UAG Setup will start the installation by adding the necessary roles and features to Windows. After adding those roles, Forefront UAG Setup will install Forefront TMG, as shown in Figure 2-7.

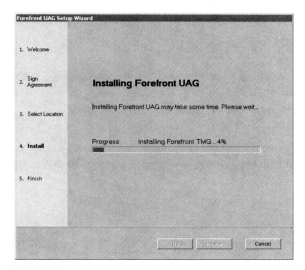

FIGURE 2-7

8. This step is the one that will probably take the most time. After finishing TMG installation, Forefront UAG Setup installs the necessary files for Forefront UAG to work. It then advances to the last page of the wizard, which offers the choice to restart the server immediately or to restart at another time, as shown in Figure 2-8.

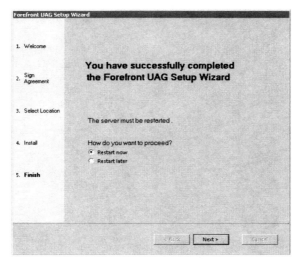

FIGURE 2-8

9. Click Next to proceed.

At this point Forefront UAG is installed; however, you will need to configure Forefront UAG network settings before you start any configuration or portal customization of the product.

Configuring Forefront UAG

Configuring network settings after installing Forefront UAG is a new step (IAG did not require this step). It uses the Getting Started Wizard to prepare the environment, so the administrator will have an experience similar to the experience of installing Forefront TMG.

> **NOTE** Keep in mind that only the external interface should have a default gateway. If your internal network has different subnets, be sure to add manual routes so that UAG can reach those remote networks.

Follow these steps to configure the network settings:

1. Click Start, All Programs, Microsoft Forefront UAG, and click Forefront UAG 2010 Management. Because this is the first time that you are using this application, the progress window shown in Figure 2-9 appears while the settings are configured.

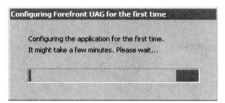

FIGURE 2-9

2. When the application is configured, the Getting Started Wizard opens and displays the Welcome page shown in Figure 2-10. It identifies three major steps for preparing Forefront UAG for use.

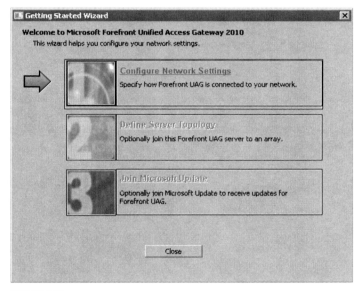

FIGURE 2-10

3. Click Configure Network Settings to start the first step of this configuration. The Welcome page of the Network Configuration Wizard, shown in Figure 2-11, appears.

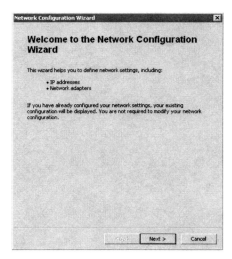

FIGURE 2-11

4. This initial step allows you to configure IP address and network adapter settings for Forefront UAG. As was previously explained, it is important to note that IP addresses need to be assigned in the Windows network configuration before Forefront UAG is installed. Click Next to proceed to the Define Network Adapters page, shown in Figure 2-12.

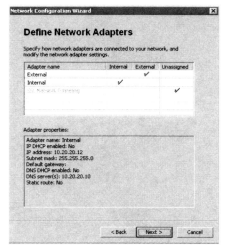

FIGURE 2-12

5. Select the Internal and External adapters based on the previously configured adapter names (the adapter names that appear in this window are retrieved from the network interfaces that are available on the operating system). To select your internal adapter, click on the row that corresponds to this adapter, and then click in the Internal column.

Follow the same steps to select the external adapter. Because there is no SSL Network Tunneling enabled yet, leave this option unassigned, and then click Next to proceed. Figure 2-13 shows the next wizard page that will appear.

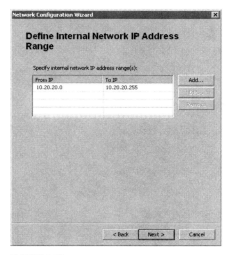

FIGURE 2-13

6. As shown in Figure 2-13, the Define Internal Network IP Address Range page allows you to define the IP range that belongs to the internal network. This is another important step. The definition should be based on your planning. When implementing Forefront UAG on a network that has multiple subnets, you need to identify to Forefront UAG all the networks that are considered internal. To add new networks, click Add, and then specify the network range. For the purpose of this example, leave the default network selected and click Next to proceed. The last page of the wizard will appear, as shown in Figure 2-14.

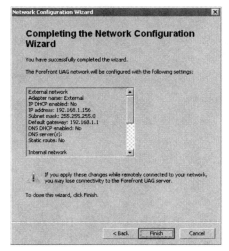

FIGURE 2-14

7. Click Finish to complete the first step of the Getting Started Wizard, and you should see an updated version of the Welcome page, as shown in Figure 2-15. The check mark indicates that the first step is complete. The arrow indicates that the next step has not yet been started.

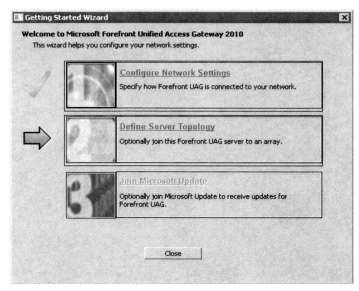

FIGURE 2-15

8. In Step Two, you define the topology in which Forefront UAG will be working. Click Define Server Topology to start this configuration. Figure 2-16 shows the first page of the Server Management Wizard.

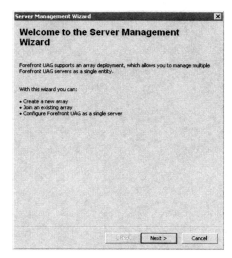

FIGURE 2-16

9. In this step, you create a new array, join to an existing array, or install a single server. Click Next and the Select Configuration page appears, as shown in Figure 2-17.

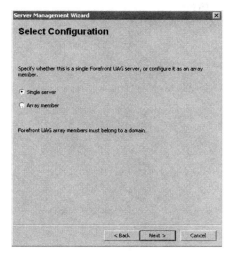

FIGURE 2-17

10. If you already have a Forefront UAG array installed, you should choose the Array Member option. In this case, leave the default option (Single Server) selected, then click Next, and the page shown in Figure 2-18 appears.

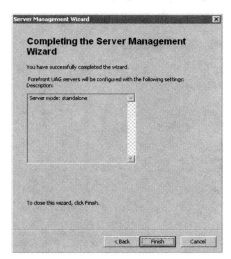

FIGURE 2-18

11. When you choose the single server option, Forefront UAG shows the Server Mode as Standalone. Click Finish to conclude this step. The Getting Started Wizard Welcome page appears again, as shown in Figure 2-19. The check marks indicate that the first

and second steps are complete. The arrow indicates that the last step has not yet been started.

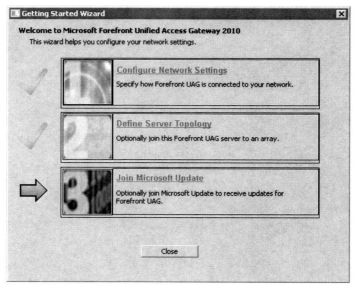

FIGURE 2-19

12. Click Join Microsoft Update to configure the way Forefront UAG will retrieve updates, and the Microsoft Update Wizard page, shown in Figure 2-20, appears.

FIGURE 2-20

13. Select the option to Use Microsoft Update When I Check For Updates (Recommended), as shown in Figure 2-20, and click OK. The wizard's Welcome page is shown again, and the check marks indicate that all steps are complete. Click Close, and the dialog box shown in Figure 2-21 appears, asking you to activate the configuration settings you have chosen.

FIGURE 2-21

14. Click Yes to start the activation, and the Activation Configuration dialog box appears, as shown in Figure 2-22.

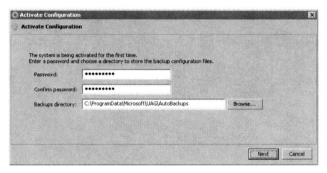

FIGURE 2-22

15. The Activate Configuration dialog box prompts you for the location in which the backup of the Forefront UAG configuration files should be stored, and also asks you to create the password that will be used for these files.

> **NOTE** This dialog box will not appear the next time you try to activate the configuration. Be sure you keep a secure record of the password and the file location.

16. Click Next to proceed, and the dialog box shown in Figure 2-23 appears.

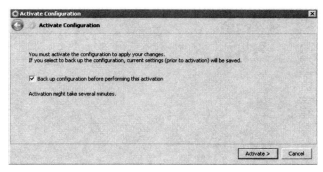

FIGURE 2-23

17. By default, the Back Up Configuration Before Performing The Activation checkbox is selected; this is the recommended setting. Click the Activate button, and Forefront UAG will commit the changes. The dialog box refreshes to show the activation progress, as shown in Figure 2-24.

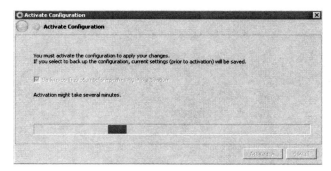

FIGURE 2-24

18. When the configuration activation is finished, the message box shown in Figure 2-25 appears. Click Finish to conclude your configuration.

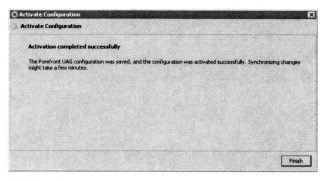

FIGURE 2-25

Now that Forefront UAG is installed, it is time to review the deployment plan and verify the application you will be publishing within your portal. Wait a minute; you still need to create your portal! You will see how to do this in the next chapter.

Deploying a Forefront UAG Array

An array is a group of Forefront UAG machines that share the same configuration. Forefront UAG arrays can have up to eight nodes, and centralized administration and the configuration for all the nodes is managed from a single location as a single entity. This capability was not available in IAG 2007. Forefront UAG arrays are based on Forefront TMG, which offers a single point (the Array Manager) for storing the configuration; the Array Manager also acts as one of the nodes of the array.

Requirements

The requirements for implementing array topology on Forefront UAG 2010 are:

- All nodes must be domain members and must belong to the same domain (an array in a workgroup is not supported).
- Array members need to be on the same Active Directory site.
- In order to add nodes to an array, you have to be the array administrator. This is a role in both Forefront UAG and Forefront TMG, so be sure that the user who is going to add the nodes is added to this role in both Forefront UAG and Forefront TMG.
- The server or servers that will be part of the array need to be added to the "Managed Server Computers" computer set in Forefront TMG, before they are added to the array.
- If there is any HTTPS trunk already created on the first Forefront UAG that was installed, be sure that the new nodes also have all the certificates that this trunk uses correctly installed.

Creating an Array

If you plan to expand your Forefront UAG deployment you can create an array. Before you create an array you should have followed the previously described installation process for all nodes of the array. Once you have done this, the next step is to create an array. The Forefront UAG server on which you perform the procedure below will become the Array Management Server (AMS) for your array.

> **NOTE** The steps below assume that there are two Forefront UAG servers already installed in your environment. In other words, the installation steps previously outlined were used on two Forefront UAG servers, which, in this case, are called UAG10 and UAG11.

Assuming that all requirements have already been met, from the first Forefront UAG node that you installed (your AMS), start the configuration by following these steps:

1. Open the Forefront UAG Management Console.
2. Click the Admin menu and choose Array Management.
3. On the Welcome To The Array Management Wizard page, click Next.
4. On the Step 1 – Configure Array Settings page, select Set This Server As The Array Manager option, as shown in Figure 2-26, and then click Next to continue.

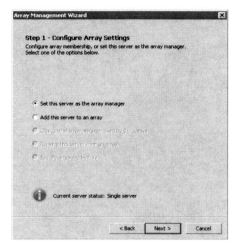

FIGURE 2-26

5. On the Step 2 – Specify Array Credentials page, type the administrator's credentials, as shown in Figure 2-27, and click Next to continue.

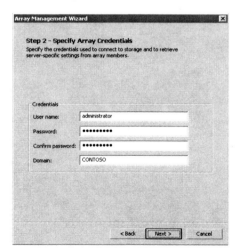

FIGURE 2-27

6. On the Step 3 – Defining Array Member Computers page, click Add, and then type the name and IP address of the other array member. Then click OK, and both nodes should appear in this page, as shown in Figure 2-28. Click Next to continue.

FIGURE 2-28

7. On the Set Server As Array Manager page, review the settings and click Finish.

8. After a few seconds a message box appears, indicating that the configuration was completed successfully. Click OK.

9. Activate the configuration by clicking Activate Options in the File menu.

> **NOTE** To confirm that this change took effect, you can open the Forefront TMG Management console, click Firewall Policy, go to Network Objects, expand Computer Sets, and open Managed Server Computers. You will see that both of the Forefront UAG nodes are shown there.

10. Open the second Forefront UAG node (in this case UAG11), and the Getting Started Wizard should appear (if this is the first time that this Forefront UAG Server is being configured). Configure the network settings.

11. The second step of the Getting Started Wizard is to define the server topology. Click Next on the first page to continue.

12. On the Select Configuration page, choose Array Member, as shown in Figure 2-29, and click Next to continue.

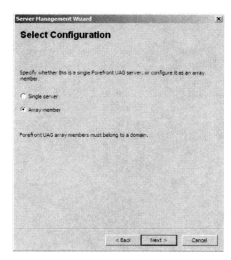

FIGURE 2-29

13. The Array Management Wizard opens automatically. Click Next to continue.

14. On the Step 1 – Configure Array Settings page, select the Add This Server To An Array option, as shown in Figure 2-30. Click Next to proceed.

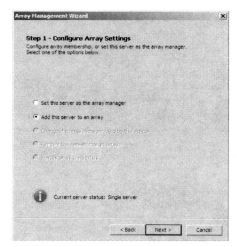

FIGURE 2-30

15. On the Step 2 – Select Array Manager page, click Browse, and then search for the Forefront UAG array manager name. When you find it, click OK, and then type the administrator's credentials, as shown in Figure 2-31. Click Next to proceed.

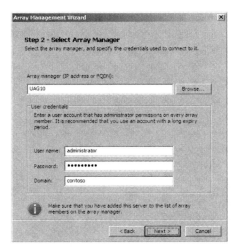

FIGURE 2-31

16. On the Joining The Array page, review the selections and click Finish. At this point, the Joining The Array process will run, and you should see the page shown in Figure 2-32.

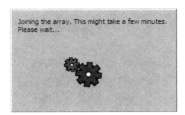

FIGURE 2-32

17. Once this process is finished, a message similar to that shown in Figure 2-33 will appear. Click OK, then click Finish.

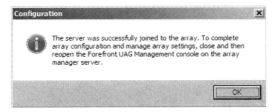

FIGURE 2-33

18. Finalize the Getting Started Wizard by running the Microsoft Update step, and select the Exit The Forefront UAG Console option to close the console.

19. To confirm that both nodes are synchronized, click Start, All Programs, Microsoft Forefront UAG, and click Forefront UAG Activation Monitor. If both nodes are synchronized, you will see a page similar to the one shown in Figure 2-34.

FIGURE 2-34

Remember that now that the array is configured, you need to configure all of the settings on the Array Manager; you can't make any changes using a Forefront UAG Management console that is installed on an array member.

Administrator's Punch List

The following key concepts and issues should be remembered and considered during the planning and deployment phase of your Forefront UAG server deployment project:

- Forefront UAG can support four access models: reverse proxy or portal, port or socket forwarding, network-level SSL VPN, and Direct Access.
- A single array can support multiple access models.
- Internet and internal name resolution infrastructures must be in place before Forefront UAG is deployed.
- A Public Key Infrastructure must be in place to support either Web site certificates or computer certificates, depending on the access model or models chosen for the array.
- Forefront UAG can be deployed in a workgroup or array. However, there are limited options for UAG deployed in a workgroup.
- DirectAccess can take advantage of an IPv6 infrastructure, but an IPv6 infrastructure is not required to deploy DirectAccess when Forefront UAG is the DirectAccess server.
- While is it expected that most enterprises will place the Forefront UAG server between a front-end and back-end firewall, this is neither a required nor a preferred configuration. Forefront UAG can be deployed with a front-end firewall only, with a back-end firewall only, or with no firewalls around it at all.

- Forefront UAG supports multicast, unicast, and IGMP multicast NLB. However, if you choose to deploy DirectAccess, you must use unicast NLB.

- NLB arrays can handle a maximum throughput of around 500Mbps.

- NLB supports NAP for endpoint detection for both portal access and DirectAccess.

- Forefront UAG should be installed on a "clean" Windows Server 2008 R2 operating system that has no other software installed and hosts no other server roles.

- You can virtualize Forefront UAG using Hyper-V on Windows Server 2008 R2 or Windows Server 2008 SP2.

- The Forefront UAG installer will install all prerequisite software; an Internet connection is not required.

- A Forefront UAG server must always have two network interfaces, no fewer and no more.

- Routing table entries should be configured on the Forefront UAG server before the Forefront UAG software is installed.

- The configuration must always be activated after changes are made to the Forefront UAG settings. Missing this step is a common reason for some features not working properly.

CHAPTER 3

Publishing Applications through Forefront UAG

■ Understanding the Publishing Mechanism on Forefront UAG   **51**

■ Publishing Exchange   **63**

■ Publishing Remote Desktop Services   **71**

■ Publishing SharePoint   **85**

Microsoft Forefront Unified Access Gateway (UAG) 2010 enables end users to have seamless experiences while accessing applications through the portal, as if they were located in the corporate network. To take full advantage of these features, it is necessary that the Forefront UAG administrator understand the full potential of this capability. In this chapter, you will learn how to create a trunk on Forefront UAG and publish applications such as Microsoft Exchange Server 2010, Windows Server 2008 Remote Desktop Services, and Microsoft SharePoint 2010.

Understanding the Publishing Mechanism on Forefront UAG

Publishing an application via Forefront UAG is the process of making the application available to external users over the Internet. One of the most powerful features that Forefront UAG inherited from its predecessor IAG is the ability to publish a wide variety of applications through the Forefront UAG portal. However, before you move further into the steps for publishing applications through Forefront UAG, it's important that you understand the way the publishing mechanism works.

When you open the Forefront UAG Management console, you will see that there are four nodes under the Forefront Unified Access Gateway tree, as shown in Figure 3-1.

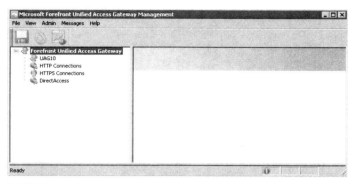

FIGURE 3-1

All applications that you want to publish through Forefront UAG need to be part of a portal, that is, part of a Web page that has all the applications that you want to make available to external users. To create a portal, you must first create a trunk, as shown in Figure 3-2. A trunk is the mechanism that Forefront UAG uses to create a portal. Every time you decide to create a portal, you will need to create a trunk first, because it is via the trunk that you can define the portal settings. The portal trunks can be either HTTP or HTTPS. If you want to create an HTTPS portal trunk, a certificate must already be installed on the Forefront UAG computer itself. The certificate needs to have the private key; otherwise, UAG will not recognize the certificate as valid, and you won't be able to create the HTTPS trunk.

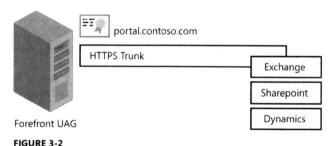

FIGURE 3-2

If you are planning to have a single portal trunk through which you will publish all applications, you will need to consider the name the certificate is going to have. You can purchase a certificate with a single name (for example, portal.contoso.com); a certificate with multiple names, also called a multiple Subject Alternative Name (SAN) certificate, with which you can assign multiple names to the same certificate; or you can use a wildcard certificate (*.contoso. com, for example).

Authentication Repository

An authentication repository is a mechanism that allows external users to authenticate against a variety of authentication directories, such as Active Directory, LDAP, Novell Directory Services, and others. By default, when you install Forefront UAG, no authentication repository is created, so you can't create a trunk that allows only authenticated users to access the applications that are published through it. Since Forefront UAG allows authentication using technologies from multiple vendors, you can create multiple authentication repositories using the parameters required by a particular technology. Figure 3-3 shows such an approach.

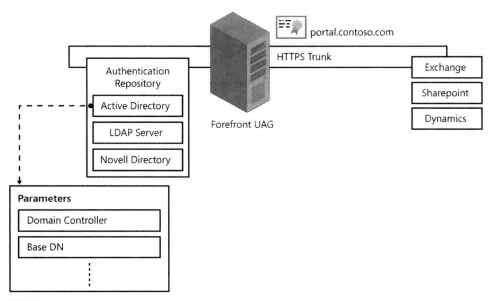

FIGURE 3-3

In this example, you will use Active Directory as the authentication repository. Complete the following steps to create this repository:

1. In the Forefront UAG Management console, click the Admin menu, and choose Authentication and Authorization Servers. When the Authentication and Authorization Servers page appears, as shown in Figure 3-4, click Add.

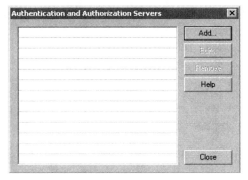

FIGURE 3-4

2. On the Add Authentication Server page, shown in Figure 3-5, in the Server Type box, select Active Directory, and then type **AD** as the Server Name. (The Server Name can be the real server name or just a name to identify the repository.) You have plenty of options, which will change according to the server type that you choose in the first field. For the purpose of this example, use Active Directory as the Server Type. The other options available are:

- **Define Domain Controllers**   Using this option, you can identify the domain controllers you are going to use for authentication.

- **Use Local Active Directory Forest Authentication**   Because Forefront UAG is domain-joined in this scenario, Use Local Active Directory Forest Authentication will make Forefront UAG use the domain controller that is available for the domain to which it is joined.

- **Base DN**   This option tells Forefront UAG where to search for users and groups when it is starting the authentication and authorization processes. For the purpose of this example, click ellipsis (…), and then, in the list, select CN=Users, DC=Contoso, DC=Com, and click OK.

- **Include Subfolders**   This option allows Forefront UAG to search not only the root (Base DN), but also the sub-containers that belong to the root. Select Include Subfolders for this example.

- **Level of Nested Groups**   This option tells Forefront UAG the level of the search it should use within the groups to which the user belongs. Using the default value zero (0) tells Forefront UAG to look only in the group to which the user directly belongs. Any value higher than zero tells Forefront UAG to search that many levels of nested groups to which the user belongs. Use 0 for this example.

- **Server Access**   Here, you will need to type the credentials for the user who will connect to Active Directory. The user needs read permission in order to perform the search.

- **Default Domain Name**   This option is available when you manually define the domain controllers that will be used for authentication. It allows you to specify the default domain to which users will log on.

The Add Authentication Server page should now look as it does in Figure 3-5.

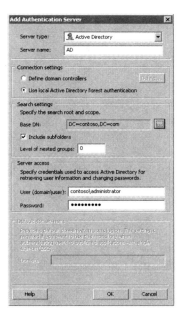

FIGURE 3-5

3. Click OK on the Add Authentication Server page. The authentication repository called AD appears on the Authentication and Authorization Servers page. Click Close to finish the creation.

4. Click File, and Activate; don't change the default backup setting; click Activate, wait until activation completes, and then click Finish.

Creating a Portal Trunk

Now that you have created an authentication repository, you can go to the next step, which is creating the portal trunk. Assuming that you already have the certificate correctly installed on Windows, use the following the steps to create a new trunk on Forefront UAG:

1. Right-click HTTPS Connections and choose New Trunk. The Create Trunk Wizard appears, as shown in Figure 3-6.

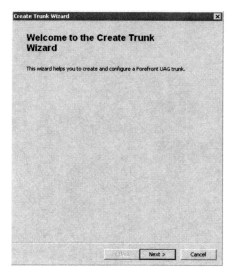

FIGURE 3-6

2. Click Next to continue. On the Step 1 – Select Trunk Type page, shown in Figure 3-7, select the trunk type. The default is to create a Portal Trunk, from which you will publish applications. The other option, ADFS Trunk, allows you to create an Active Directory Federation Server trunk for federation services. For this particular example leave the default option selected, as shown in Figure 3-7, and click Next to proceed.

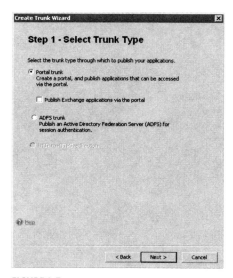

FIGURE 3-7

3. On the Step 2 – Setting The Trunk page, shown in Figure 3-8, you set up the Trunk Name (no space), the public name (in this case, **portal.contoso.com**), and the information regarding the external Web site, including the IP address that will be used by this trunk and the ports that will be used by HTTP and HTTPS protocols. For the purpose of this example, use the options shown in Figure 3-8, and click Next to proceed.

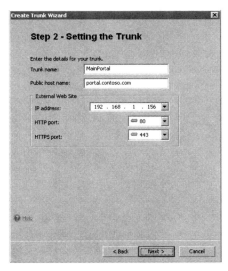

FIGURE 3-8

> **NOTE** If you are using NLB, Step 2 will be slightly different because it will reflect the NLB settings.

4. On the Step 3 – Authentication page, shown in Figure 3-9, click Add, highlight the authentication repository that you created earlier, and click Select. Use the default values for the other options and click Next to proceed.

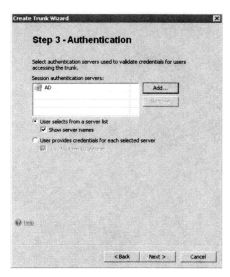

FIGURE 3-9

5. On the Step 4 – Certificate page, shown in Figure 3-10, select the certificate that will be used by this trunk. The certificates that appear in this list are the ones that are correctly installed on Windows. For the purpose of this example select the certificate Portal.contoso.com.

FIGURE 3-10

6. On the Step 5 – Endpoint Security page, shown in Figure 3-11, choose whether Forefront UAG or Network Access Protection (NAP) will manage the Endpoint Security policy. For the purpose of this example, leave the default option selected and click Next to continue.

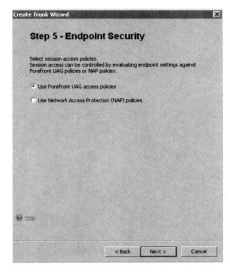

FIGURE 3-11

NOTE If you select NAP Policies in the Endpoint Security step, you need a NAP Server that is already configured with the NAP policies, because Forefront UAG will rely on it to validate the user's health state.

7. Since you selected Forefront UAG to manage the endpoint security policies, the next step is to specify the endpoint policies for non-privileged (guests) and for privileged (company's users) users. On the Step 6 – Endpoint Policies page, shown in Figure 3-12, leave the default options selected, and click Next to proceed.

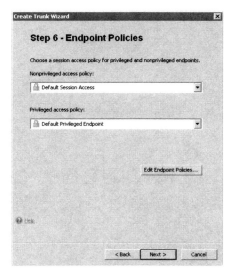

FIGURE 3-12

NOTE For more information about ways to design an endpoint security policy, read the "Endpoint Component Deployment Design Guide" white paper. You can download it from *http://download.microsoft.com/download/D/8/6/D86817B8-29C8-45DB-AFBC -054A00B8BCDF/ComponentPlanning.docx.*

8. On the Completing The Create Trunk Wizard page, click Finish.
9. Click File, Activate, leave the default backup setting selected, click Activate, wait until it activates, and then click Finish.

Client Experience

At this point, the portal is created but it is empty. There is no application on it, but you can still open the portal and validate the two settings that should now be working: authentication and responsiveness on port 443. To perform these validations, complete the following steps:

1. At an external workstation, click Start, type **https://portal.contoso.com**, and then press Enter.
2. If the root CA is not trusted by the external client, you will receive a message asking if you want to proceed even though the certificate was issued by non-trusted entity. Click Continue To This Website to proceed.
3. Forefront UAG will start downloading the client components. Depending on your browser configuration, you might see the screen shown in Figure 3-13, in which you

have an alert in the information bar asking whether to allow the Web site to install Forefront UAG. Right-click each information bar and choose the Install This Add-on for All Users on This Computer option.

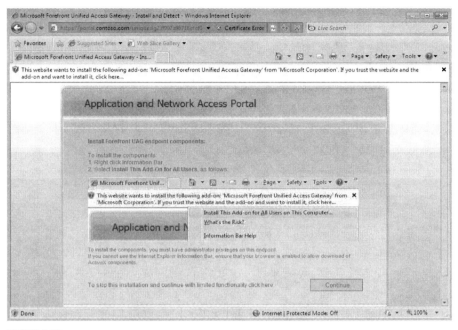

FIGURE 3-13

4. Once you allow the add-on to install, the Forefront UAG portal will prompt you with the dialog box shown in Figure 3-14. Click Install to proceed.

FIGURE 3-14

5. If you have pop-up blocker enabled on your browser, a warning about endpoint components will appear, as shown in Figure 3-15. Click Yes to add the site to the pop-up blocker's list of allowed sites and proceed.

FIGURE 3-15

6. Because the certificate was issued by a non-trusted entity, from the client's perspective, a Security Alert appears, as shown in Figure 3-16. Choose the Trust This Site option, select Temporarily, Until I Disconnect From This Site, and then click Trust to proceed.

FIGURE 3-16

7. On the Authentication page, type the credentials in the SAM format (domain\user) and click Log On. The portal page will appear, as shown in Figure 3-17.

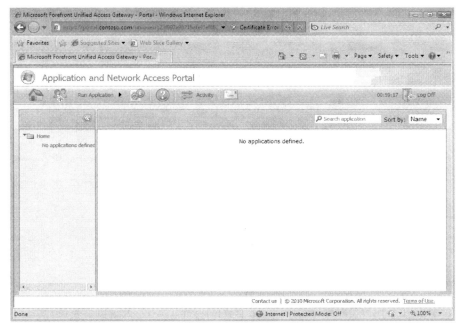

FIGURE 3-17

8. Because there is no application published through the portal yet, the right pane is empty (except for the note No Applications Defined), but take some time to familiarize yourself with the portal page, and then click Log Off to close the portal.

Publishing Exchange

The first application that you will publish through the Forefront UAG portal is Exchange. As you know, Exchange offers three core services for external users: mail Web access via App, Outlook client access via Outlook Anywhere, and mobile access via Exchange Active Sync. Forefront UAG allows you to publish all those services through the portal, and you will do that for this example. Forefront UAG allows you to publish different versions of Exchange Server; for the purpose of this example you are going to use Microsoft Exchange 2010.

Before you start configuring Exchange publishing through Forefront UAG, it is important to review the following items in your Exchange infrastructure:

- Confirm that these the Exchange services are working internally. If they are not, then troubleshoot the problems and ensure that the services are working.

- Gather Exchange Server identification information, such as the server's name and IP Address.

- Validate the authentication method used by Outlook Web App (Basic, NTLM, or Forms), by Outlook Anywhere (Basic, NTLM, or Kerberos), and by Active Sync (Basic,

NTLM, or Kerberos). You will need to adjust Forefront UAG based on the particular authentication method that those services are using.

■ Check the connectivity and name resolution between Forefront UAG Server and Exchange Server.

Now that you have gathered all the information necessary to start configuring Exchange services, complete the following steps to publish Exchange through Forefront UAG:

1. In the Forefront UAG Management console, select MainPortal, then, under Application Name, Applications, right-click Portal, and then choose Add. The Step 1 – Select Application page appears, as shown in Figure 3-18. Under the Web option, select Microsoft Exchange Server (all versions), and click Next to proceed.

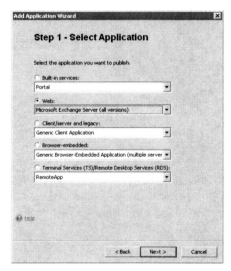

FIGURE 3-18

2. On the Step 2 – Select Exchange Services page, shown in Figure 3-19, click the Exchange Version drop-down list, choose Microsoft Exchange Server 2010, and select all three services. Click Next to proceed.

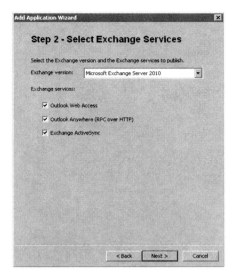

FIGURE 3-19

3. In the Step 3 – Configure Application page, shown in Figure 3-20, type **Exchange** in the Application Name box, and click Next.

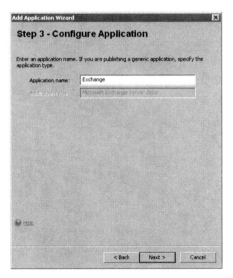

FIGURE 3-20

4. On the Step 4 – Select Endpoint Policies page, shown in Figure 3-21, you choose the endpoint policies. For the purpose of this example, leave the default options selected, and click Next to proceed.

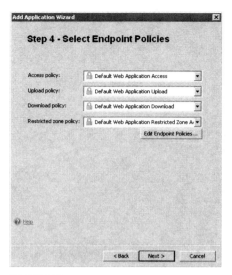

FIGURE 3-21

5. On the Step 5 – Deploying an Application page, shown in Figure 3-22, you have a chance to specify whether the Exchange Server in which you are publishing is located in a single server or in a farm. Usually, in high availability scenarios, the Exchange Client Access Server (CAS) is part of a farm that contains multiple servers. If that's the case, you need to select the second option, Configure A Farm Of Application Servers. For the purpose of this example, leave Configure An Application Server selected, and click Next to proceed.

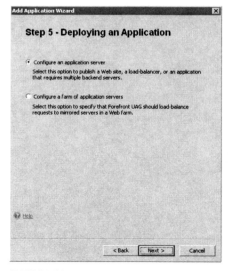

FIGURE 3-22

6. On the Step 6 – Web Servers page, shown in Figure 3-23, type the identification information about the Exchange Server that you collected earlier. In the Addresses box, type the Exchange server name, confirm the Port used by the internal Exchange server (in this case, HTTPS 443), and type the Public Host Name that external users will be using to connect to the portal. Click Next to proceed.

FIGURE 3-23

7. On the Step 7 – Authentication page, shown in Figure 3-24, select the authentication repository that was created earlier. Click Add, highlight AD, and click Select. In the lower part of the window, you can select the way Forefront UAG will interact with the Exchange server from the authentication standpoint. By default, the Both option is selected; it means that Forefront UAG will be able to authenticate whether it receives an HTTP 401 from the Exchange or an HTML form. Click Next to continue.

FIGURE 3-24

8. The authentication method selected in the previous page is going to be used by the Outlook Web Access (OWA) service; however, Outlook Anywhere and Exchange Active Sync don't use the same authentication method. Therefore, when you click Next, the configuration warning shown in Figure 3-25 will appear. This warning is just to remind you that those two types of clients will be using either Basic or NTLM authentication. Click Yes to continue.

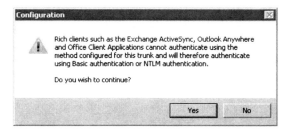

FIGURE 3-25

9. On the Step 8 – Outlook Anywhere page, shown in Figure 3-26, make your selection according to the authentication schema that is being used on Exchange. The authentication method used by Exchange server is information that you should have collected prior to start the configuration, during the planning phase. For the purpose of this example, choose Use Basic Authentication for Outlook Anywhere and choose No Authentication for Autodiscover, as shown in Figure 3-26.

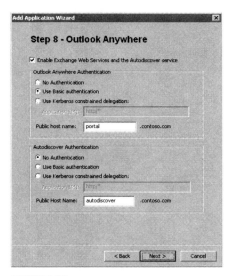

FIGURE 3-26

This page also contains the following options for Outlook Anywhere and Autodiscover:

- **No Authentication** This option allows anonymous access; it doesn't require authentication.

- **Use Kerberos Constrained Delegation** This option enables published Web servers to re-authenticate users by Kerberos, after their identity has been verified by Forefront UAG using a non-Kerberos authentication method. When selecting this option you will have to ensure that there is an application Service Principal Name (SPN) setup on Active Directory that matches the value here.

- **Public Host Name** This option lets you set the public name that will be used by this application.

10. On the Step 8 – Portal Link page, shown in Figure 3-27, you can specify the way the application appears in the portal when the user connects to it. The Portal Name allows you to specify a friendly name for the application. The Application URL specifies the internal link for the server that you want to access. Click Next to continue.

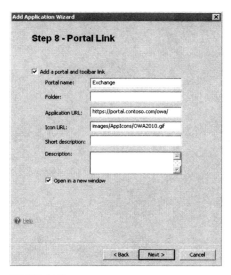

FIGURE 3-27

NOTE In the product, Step 9 is misnumbered as a second Step 8. We recognize that it is an error, but we have reproduced it here to mirror what you will see.

11. On the Step 10 – Authorization page, shown in Figure 3-28, you can select the users who will be able to access this application through the portal. For the purpose of this example, leave the default Authorize All Users selected, and click Next to continue.

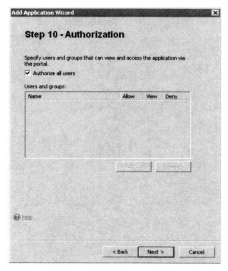

FIGURE 3-28

12. Click Finish to complete this wizard.

13. Click File, click Activate, leave the default backup option selection, click Activate, and wait until it activates. When it is activated, the warning shown in Figure 3-29 will appear. Read it carefully.

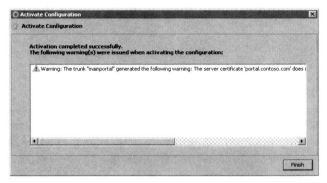

FIGURE 3-29

You receive this warning because you are using a certificate that has one name (portal.contoso.com). By default, the autodiscover feature appends its name to the domain, creating the external path called autodiscover.contoso.com, so the certificate doesn't match this name. To fix this problem you need to either acquire a SAN Certificate that contains all the domain names that you want to authenticate, including the autodiscover name, or use a wildcard certificate. Click Finish to conclude the Wizard.

14. Once you acquire the new certificate, you need to install it on Windows, and then change the portal trunk to use it. To change the certificate in the portal trunk, under Trunk Configuration, click Configure. On the Server Certificate drop-down list, choose the new certificate, click OK, and then activate again.

Publishing Remote Desktop Services

As the name Unified Access Gateway suggests, Forefront UAG aims to be the central solution from which you can enable remote access to applications and services on your network, regardless of the type of device the user uses to connect. Forefront UAG can provide access in a number of ways, as you've seen in the earlier example of Exchange Services publishing.

Another key scenario for UAG is publishing Remote Desktop Services. In the past, if you wanted to publish a terminal server to Internet users, you needed to allow inbound access to TCP port 3389 (by default) to the terminal server. This led to several problems, including:

■ If you needed to publish multiple terminal servers on their default ports, then you needed an IP address on the network gateway for each of the terminal servers.

- Internet-based clients might be located behind firewalls or Web proxy devices that don't allow outbound access to TCP port 3389. This would prevent the terminal services client from connecting to the corporate terminal server.

- There was no granular access control over who could connect to a terminal server, and the terminal server represented an Internet-facing device. This made publishing a terminal server a security risk, because of the enormous "attacker surface" to which the terminal server was exposed.

A solution to these problems is the Remote Desktop Gateway (RD Gateway). RD Gateway allows Remote Desktop Clients to use HTTPS to connect to the published servers using Remote Desktop Services. Actually, the protocol works in a way similar to the RPC/HTTP protocol: The Remote Desktop Protocol (RDP) communication is encapsulated in an RPC header, which is then encapsulated in an HTTP header, which is then encrypted using SSL. When the communication reaches the RD Gateway, the gateway decrypts the sessions, removes the HTTP header, removes the RPC header, and forwards the RDP communication to the Remote Desktop Server.

The RD Gateway solves the problems described earlier, because it allows you to:

- Publish multiple Remote Desktop Session Host (RD Session Host) servers using a single RD Gateway or connection broker.

- Connect even if outbound TCP 3389 is not available, because the only requirement is that outbound TCP 443 is available. TCP 443 is almost universally available, and the RDC client can connect to the RD Gateway even when a Web proxy is used to access the Internet.

- Control the users who can access Remote Desktop Services and the RD Session Host servers to which they can connect.

Remote Desktop Services included with Windows Server 2008 and Windows Server 2008 R2 allow you to publish either an entire desktop or selected applications only. Applications published using Remote Desktop Services are referred to as RemoteApp programs. When users connect to RemoteApp programs, they access only the application using Remote Desktop Connection (RDC), and the application appears to be in a normal application window. The user experience is the same with a RemoteApp program as it is with a locally installed application. RemoteApp enables you to provide "least privilege" access by giving users access to the applications they need to perform their work, but nothing more.

Forefront UAG can host the RD Gateway role service, which allows you to remove the RD Gateway role from other servers on your network and aggregate your remote access configuration and monitoring on a single server or array. The RD Gateway functionality included with Forefront UAG is supported in both single server and array configurations, and you can add high availability to the configuration by enabling NLB on the Forefront UAG RD Gateway array.

During the RDC client connection to the UAG server or array:

1. The user connects to the Forefront UAG portal using a Web browser.

2. The user logs into the portal to confirm the user's identity. Endpoint detection takes place to determine the level of access the user should have, based on who the user is and any custom configuration being used.

3. A link to a session-based desktop or RemoteApp program is presented to the user in the portal. The user clicks a link to start the application.

4. The portal uses an ActiveX control to turn on the RDC client software on the user's computer. When the ActiveX control turns on the RDC client, the client will start based on parameters determined during the endpoint detection process. For example, based on endpoint detection, it might be determined that clipboard data should not be available to the user.

5. The RDC client begins an RDP/HTTPS session with the RD Gateway server on the Forefront UAG server. Forefront UAG verifies that the user logged onto the portal and has a session cookie. Then the RD Gateway accepts the connection and forwards it to the RDS host behind the Forefront UAG server.

Why Use Forefront UAG to Publish Remote Desktop Services?

Forefront UAG provides an option for RDS publishing. However, a good question to ask is: Why would one use Forefront UAG to publish Remote Desktop Services rather than deploying a dedicated RD Gateway solution? The reasons include:

- **Strong authentication methods** Users must authenticate to the portal before they are allowed access to Remote Desktop Services applications. Forefront UAG enables a wide array of single- and multi-factor authentication options that aren't available if you use RD Gateway without Forefront UAG.

- **Pre-authentication** You can prevent anonymous attacks because all users must be able to authenticate to the portal before reaching the RD Gateway.

- **Access control and endpoint detection** When you publish RDS using Forefront UAG, you have more granular control over what users can do in the RDP session, based on the results of endpoint detection. For example, if a user connects from an untrusted machine, you can prevent access to drive mappings, printers, or the shared clipboard. You can use either the integrated endpoint detection included with Forefront UAG or take advantage of NAP. Also, depending on the user or computer status, you can block access to select session-based desktops or RemoteApp programs in the portal.

- **A Single Point of Access and Control** You can configure a Forefront UAG server or array as your central RD Gateway point of access and control. When you configure a Forefront UAG RD Gateway array, you configure the RD Gateway settings on the array master, and the configuration is automatically applied to all members of the array. In addition, you can take advantage of NLB to make the array highly available.

Publishing RemoteApp Programs

There are two ways you can publish Remote Desktop services: publish entire desktops or publish RemoteApp programs. When you publish RemoteApp programs, the application is made available to the user over an RDP connection; the user does not need the application installed locally. There are many advantages to this approach, such as the ability to make the application available to users who don't have access to the application installation files and the ability to centralize application access to improve application metering and reporting.

The following procedure describes the way to publish RemoteApp programs in a UAG portal. The procedure assumes that you have already created the portal and you now want to enable remote access to RemoteApp programs.

1. On the RD Session Host server, open the Administrative Tools menu and select the RemoteApp Manager console.

2. Confirm that you have added the RemoteApp programs that you want to publish and that they appear in the console, as shown in Figure 3-30. Note that if you add RemoteApp programs in the future, you will need to repeat this process.

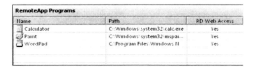

FIGURE 3-30

3. In the Actions pane, click the Export RemoteApp Settings link, as shown in Figure 3-31.

FIGURE 3-31

4. In the Export RemoteApp Settings dialog box, select the Export The RemoteApp Programs List And Settings To A File option and click OK, as shown in Figure 3-32.

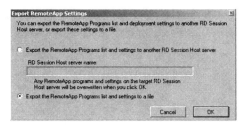

FIGURE 3-32

5. In the Save As dialog box, choose a location in which to save the .tspub file, and click Save. Click OK in the dialog box that says that the settings were successfully exported. In the Applications section of the console, click Add.

6. At the Forefront UAG server, open the Forefront UAG Management console, select the portal you want to use to publish the RemoteApp programs, and click Add, as shown in Figure 3-33.

FIGURE 3-33

7. On the Welcome To The Add Application Wizard page, click Next.

8. On the Step 1 – Select Application page, select the Terminal Services (TS)/Remote Desktop Services (RDS) option. From the drop-down list, select the RemoteApp option, as shown in Figure 3-34, and click Next.

FIGURE 3-34

9. On the Step 2 – Configure Application page, type a name for the application in the Application Name box. In this example, **Remote Applications** is used, as shown in Figure 3-35. Click Next.

FIGURE 3-35

10. On the Select Endpoint Policies page, you will choose from a number of options:
   - In the Access Policy drop-down box, select a policy with which endpoints must comply to access published RemoteApp programs in the portal.
   - In the Printers, Clipboard, and Drives drop-down lists, select the access policies with which endpoints must comply in order to access these resources during the remote desktop sessions.
   - If the portal is configured to use NAP and you have a Network Policy Server configured, you need to do the following (note that the example portal in this exercise is not NAP-enabled):
     - Select Require Network Access Protection (NAP) Compliance, to specify that only those endpoints that comply with NAP policy can access published RemoteApp programs.
     - Select Require NAP Compliance For RDS Device Redirection Only, to specify that only those endpoints that comply with NAP policy can access RDS server devices and resources such as drives, printers, and the clipboard. Access to other resources and application on an RDS server does not require NAP compliance.
     - If you do not require clients to use NAP to access the published RemoteApp programs, select Do Not Require NAP Compliance.

11. Confirm that the Use RDS Single Sign-On (SSO) Services checkbox is selected, as shown in Figure 3-36. When SSO is enabled for the session, the client passes the SSO credentials to RDS for authentication and access. Click Next.

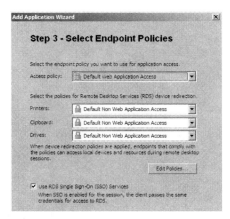

FIGURE 3-36

12. On the Step 4 – Import RemoteApp Programs page, click Browse to locate the .tspub file you exported for the RD Session Host server. Note that when you import the file, it automatically fills in the RD Session Host Or RD Connection Broker (IP address Or FQDN) box, as shown in Figure 3-37. If you have RD Connection Brokers, you can enter the IP addresses or FQDNs of the Connection Brokers in the IP Addresses, IP Address Ranges, FQDNs, Or Subnets box. Click Next.

FIGURE 3-37

13. On the Step 5 – Select Publishing Type page, select an application in the Available RemoteApps section on the left, and then click the double arrow to move the application into the Published RemoteApps section. Figure 3-38 shows the result of this action. Click Next.

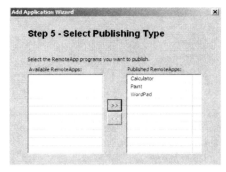

FIGURE 3-38

14. On the Step 6 – Configure Client Settings page, choose the Display Resolution and Display Colors you want to be available to the clients, as shown in Figure 3-39. You can use the default setting, which uses the imported settings that were configured on the RD Session Host server, or you can set your own custom display resolution and display colors by choosing them from the drop-down boxes. Click Next.

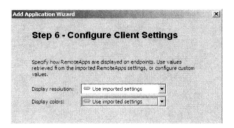

FIGURE 3-39

15. On the Step 7 – Portal Link page, leave the option to add a portal and toolbar link selected and click Next.

16. On the Step 8 – Authorization page, you can choose the default setting, which is Authorize All Users, as shown in Figure 3-40, or you can disable that option and click Add to add custom users or groups who are allowed access to these RemoteApp programs.

FIGURE 3-40

17. On the Completing The Add Application Wizard page, click Finish.

18. In the Applications section of the console, you can see the new Remote Applications entry, as shown in Figure 3-41.

FIGURE 3-41

19. Click Activate Configuration. In the Activate Configuration box, click Activate. When the activation completes, click Finish.

Publishing an Administrator-Controlled Remote Desktop

The second way to make remote applications available to users is by publishing entire session-based desktop environments. There are two ways you can do this with the Forefront UAG RD Gateway. The first method enables you to publish access to a pre-defined, administrator-determined RD Session Host server. The second method enables the user to choose and then connect to an RD Session Host server.

The following procedure describes the way to publish an administrator-defined RD Session Host server. The RD Session Host server will be published within a portal that has already been created and will be added to that portal.

1. In the Forefront UAG console, in the Applications area, click Add, as shown in Figure 3-42.

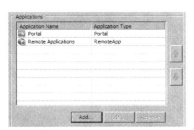

FIGURE 3-42

2. On the Welcome To The Add Application Wizard page, click Next.

3. On the Step 1 – Select Application page, select the Terminal Services (TS)/Remote Desktop Services (RDS) option. Select the Remote Desktop (Predefined) option from the drop-down list, as shown in Figure 3-43. Click Next.

FIGURE 3-43

4. On the Step 2 – Configure Application page, type a name for the application in the Application Name box, as shown in Figure 3-44. For this example, type **Predefined Desktop**, and click Next.

FIGURE 3-44

5. On the Step 3 – Select Endpoint Policies page, you will see the same selections described in the "Publishing RemoteApp Applications" section earlier in this chapter. Choose the policies for your application, and then click Next.

6. On the Step 4 – Configure Server Settings page, in the RD Session Host Or RD Connection Broker (IP Address Or FQDN) box, enter the name of the RD Session Host server you want to publish. For this example, enter **rds.contoso.com**, as shown in Figure 3-45. If you have a Connection Broker, you can enter the IP addresses, IP address ranges, or FQDNs for those connection brokers in the IP Addresses, IP Address Ranges, FQDNs, Or Subnets box. Click Next.

FIGURE 3-45

7. On the Step 5 – Configure Client Settings page, you can configure the Display Resolution and Display Colors available to the users, as shown in Figure 3-46. The default settings are full screen resolution and 32-bit color. However, you can use the options in the drop-down lists to define these settings for your users. Click Next.

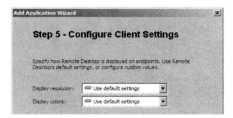

FIGURE 3-46

8. On the Step 6 – Portal Link page, accept the default settings and click Next.

9. On the Step 7 – Authorization page, the default setting is Authorize All Users, as shown in Figure 3-47. If you don't want to authorize all users, you can remove the check mark from the Authorize All Users checkbox, and then click Add to define custom users or groups to which you want to provide this application. Click Next.

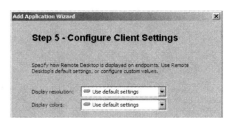

FIGURE 3-47

10. On the Completing The Add Application Wizard page, click Finish.

11. The new application will appear in the Applications section in the portal, as shown in Figure 3-48.

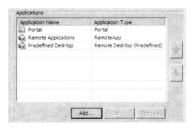

FIGURE 3-48

12. Click Activate Configuration, and then on the Activate Configuration dialog box, click Activate.

13. On the Activate Configuration page, click Finish.

Publishing User-Defined Desktops

In addition to being able to publish administrator-defined desktops, you can also publish desktops from which users can choose. For example, you might have a collection of RD Session Host servers that host different applications, and users connect to the RD Session Host server that hosts the applications they require. Or you might assign some RD Session Host servers to developers and other RD Session Host servers to knowledge workers. The developers choose the RD Session Host server they need and the knowledge workers choose the RD Session Host server appropriate for them.

The following procedures describe the way to publish user-defined RD Session Host servers. Note that a portal has already been created and the user-defined RD Session Host server application is added to this existing portal.

1. In the Forefront UAG console, in the applications area, click Add, as shown in Figure 3-49.

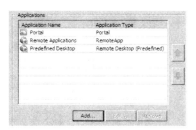

FIGURE 3-49

2. On the Welcome To The Add Application Wizard page, click Next.

3. On the Step 1 – Select Application page, select the Terminal Services (TS)/Remote Desktop Services (RDS) option. Select the Remote Desktop (User Defined) option from the drop-down list, as shown in Figure 3-50. Click Next.

FIGURE 3-50

4. On the Step 2 – Configure Application page, type a name for the application in the Application Name box. For this example type **User Chooses RDS Server**, as shown in Figure 3-51, and click Next.

FIGURE 3-51

5. On the Step 3 – Select Endpoint Policies page, you will see the selections described in the "Publishing RemoteApp Applications" section earlier in this chapter. Choose the policies for your application, and then click Next.

6. On the Step 4 – Configure Server Settings page, in the IP Addresses, IP Address Ranges, FQDNs, Or Subnets page, type the names of the servers from which you want your users to choose, as shown in Figure 3-52. When users select this application, they will be able to enter the name of the server to which they want to connect. If that server name is included in the list on this page, a connection will be established; if the server name the user enters is not in this list, the user will see an error dialog box indicating that the server isn't available.

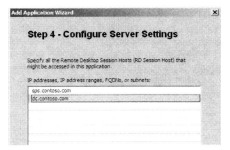

FIGURE 3-52

7. On the Step 5 – Configure Client Settings page, you can configure the Display Resolution and Display Colors available to the users. For the purpose of this example, keep the default settings, which are full screen resolution and 32-bit color, as shown in Figure 3-53. However, you can use the options in the drop-down lists to define these settings for your user. Click Next.

FIGURE 3-53

8. On the Step 6 – Portal Link page, accept the default settings and click Next.

9. On the Step 7 – Authorization page, the default setting is Authorize All Users, which is the option used in this example, as shown in Figure 3-54. If you don't want to authorize all users, you can clear the Authorize All Users checkbox, and then click Add to add the names of custom users or groups to whom you want to provide this application. Click Next.

FIGURE 3-54

10. On the Completing The Add Application Wizard page, click Finish.

11. The new application will appear in the Applications section in the portal, as shown in Figure 3-55.

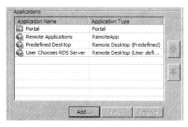

FIGURE 3-55

12. Click Activate Configuration on the toolbar. In the Activate Configuration dialog box, click Activate.

13. On the Activate Configuration page, click Finish.

> **NOTE** For more information on Remote Desktop Services publishing using Forefront UAG, please see the "Remote Desktop Services Publishing Solution Guide," at *http://www.microsoft.com/downloads/details.aspx?FamilyID=D192C703-E30B-4D47 -9992-12B84C7554CB&displaylang=en&displaylang=en.*

Publishing SharePoint

In addition to being the ideal solution for publishing Exchange and Remote Desktop Services, Forefront UAG is the best solution for publishing Microsoft SharePoint-technology-based sites. This includes Windows SharePoint Services, Microsoft SharePoint Server 2007, and Microsoft SharePoint 2010. Forefront UAG provides three application templates you can use right out of the box to publish your SharePoint sites:

■ **Microsoft SharePoint Server 2010** This template provides support for Alternate Access Mappings (AAM). This enables UAG to provide a high-fidelity SharePoint 2010 experience for users who are accessing the site through the Forefront UAG server.

■ **Microsoft Office SharePoint Server 2007** Like the SharePoint 2010 template, this template provides access to Alternate Access Mappings, so that users have full SharePoint functionality when accessing the SharePoint sites through the Forefront UAG portal.

■ **Office SharePoint Portal Server 2003 and Windows SharePoint Services 3.0** This template uses the Forefront UAG Host Address Translation feature to provide a rich SharePoint experience to users accessing the site through the portal.

Why Use Forefront UAG as a SharePoint Publishing Solution?

There are a number of methods you can use to publish SharePoint sites. For example, Microsoft Threat Management Gateway (TMG) 2010 provides a SharePoint publishing wizard that makes it easy to publish SharePoint sites. There are also other reverse proxy and SSL VPN applications that you can use to publish SharePoint sites and applications. Given the number of options available to you, why use Forefront UAG?

Some of the reasons that Forefront UAG is the preferred SharePoint publishing solution include:

- **Information leakage protection**   Forefront UAG enables the client system to clean up after itself after a portal session. After connecting to SharePoint, the endpoint clean-up feature deletes cached files, cookies, temporary files, and other information that could lead to information leakage.

- **Web farm load balancing**   Web farm load balancing (WFLB) allows you to publish a farm of SharePoint servers, which removes the need to use NLB on the Web farm and the need to use an expensive and single-point-of-failure hardware load balancer. It's important to note that the Forefront TMG 2010 SharePoint publishing solution also supports WFLB.

- **Expanded authentication methods**   One of the unique advantages of Forefront UAG is that it supports an almost unlimited number of authentication providers and authentication options for accessing the portal.

- **Single sign on for SharePoint and OWA access**   When users log into the Forefront UAG portal and access the SharePoint server, the same credentials that are used to access the portal can be used to access Exchange Web services, so users can move seamlessly between OWA and SharePoint without re-authentication. It's important to note that the same capabilities are available with Forefront TMG 2010.

- **Simplified Portal Experience**   Users appreciate the SSL VPN portal experience, because all of their applications are available in a single interface. They don't need to remember multiple URLs to access the applications they need to accomplish their work.

- **Custom time out protection**   UAG supports portal and application time outs, based on the results of endpoint detection. Different time out values can be assigned based on the level of trust assigned to the endpoint.

- **Advanced application layer inspection**   Forefront UAG employs both positive and negative logic filtering. The positive logic filtering allows only known good communications to reach the SharePoint site, while the negative logic filtering prevents known bad communications from being passed to the SharePoint site.

- **Policy-based access**   You can assign situation-specific levels of access to users when they are connecting to the SharePoint site. For example, if the user is connecting from a low-trust computer, such as a kiosk, you can block the user's ability to upload docu-ments to the SharePoint site, even if that user can upload documents from a trusted home computer.

Forefront UAG Web Site Certificate Requirements

The Forefront UAG portal site requires a certificate when you configure the portal. Defining the portal certificate requires some advance planning, such as considering the name that will be used by external clients, the certificates that are already in place in your environment, and your DNS configuration. In general, there are two types of certificates you can use on a Forefront UAG portal:

- **Wildcard certificates**

    A wildcard certificate uses the wildcard value "*" in the host name of the FQDN included in the subject or common name assigned to the certificate. For example, if you want to publish applications that belong to the contoso.com domain, you can obtain and install a certificate with the subject or common name *.contoso.com. The wildcard certificate enables a high level of compatibility and reduces the risk of some publishing scenarios not working correctly, but you need to be careful of client applications that do not accept wildcard certificates. The wildcard at the left of the FQDN can represent a host name or any number of subdomains under the domain named in the certificate. For example, if you had a wildcard certificate with the *.contoso.com subject or common name, it would be valid for requests for *www.contoso.com* and *www.na.contoso.com*.

- **Subject Alternative Name (SAN) Certificates**

    A certificate can contain a subject name and then any number of subject alternative names. When configuring subject alternative names, make sure that the first SAN you create is the same as the common name. After that, you can include any number of SAN entries on the certificate. If you want the Forefront UAG server to answer to mul-tiple site names, you can include those site names as subject alternative names. Be sure that your client applications can recognize and use the SAN entries. In addition, if you need to support additional site names at a later date, you will need to acquire a new certificate and bind that to the Forefront UAG portal.

The certificate you use for the portal is a typical Web site certificate that can be used for server authentication. If you use the Windows Certificate Server, the default Web site certifi-cate template will work with Forefront UAG portals. Forefront UAG accesses certificates stored in the Certificates\Personal store in the local machine certificate store. Be sure that the private key is included with the certificate; otherwise, the certificate will not work for application and portal publishing.

Publishing a Simple Windows SharePoint Services 3.0 Web Site

Forefront UAG can publish multiple versions of SharePoint, including Windows SharePoint Services 3.0, SharePoint Server 2007, and SharePoint Server 2010. In the following example, you will see the way to use Forefront UAG to publish a single Windows SharePoint Services 3.0 site, installed on Windows Server 2008 R2. If you choose to replicate this example configuration, be aware that you need to install Windows SharePoint Services 3.0 SP2 on Windows Server 2008 R2. Earlier versions of Windows SharePoint Services will not install on Windows Server 2008 R2.

The following steps demonstrate the way to publish a Windows SharePoint Services 3.0 Web site:

1. In the Forefront UAG Management console, in the Applications frame, click Add, as shown in Figure 3-56.

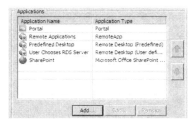

FIGURE 3-56

2. On the Welcome To The Add Application Wizard page, click Next.

3. On the Step 1 – Select Application page (as shown in Figure 3-57), select the Web option. From the drop-down list, select the Microsoft Office SharePoint Portal Server 2003 option. Click Next.

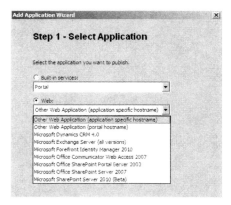

FIGURE 3-57

4. On the Step 2 – Configure Application page, enter the name of the application in the Application Name box. For this example, type **SharePoint Services**, as shown in Figure 3-58. Click Next to continue.

FIGURE 3-58

5. On the Step 3 – Select Endpoint Policies page, leave the default options selected and click Next.

6. On the Step 4 – Deploying an Application page, select the Configure An Application Server option, as shown in Figure 3-59, and click Next.

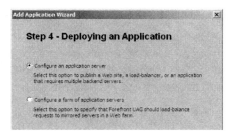

FIGURE 3-59

7. On the Step 5 – Web Servers page, type the name of the SharePoint server you want to publish in the Addresses box. In this example, the name of the SharePoint server is **sps.contoso.com**, as shown in Figure 3-60. Click Next.

FIGURE 3-60

8. On the Step 6 – Authentication page, confirm that the Use Single Sign-On To Send Credentials To Published Applications checkbox is selected, to enable SSO for applica-

tions published within the portal. Click Add to select an authentication server. In this example, you are using the Active Directory authentication server dc.contoso.com, as shown in Figure 3-61. Accept the default client authentication method, which is Both. Click Next.

FIGURE 3-61

9. On the Step 7 – Portal Link page, accept the default settings and click Next.

10. On the Step 8 – Authorization page, the Authorize All Users checkbox is enabled by default; it allows all authenticated users to access the SharePoint application. If you want to allow only a subset of authenticated users to access the application, clear the Authorize All Users checkbox, and click Add to add the names of custom users and groups. Click Next.

11. On the Completing The Add Application Wizard page, click Finish.

12. Click Activate Application. On the Activate Configuration page, click Activate. Click Finish when the activation completes.

Validating the Configuration

A number of steps were used to publish the RD Gateway and SharePoint applications. Let's see whether the applications published through Forefront UAG are accessible to a client on an external network.

The first step is to point the browser to the URL for the portal. When your users reach the portal, they will see the logon page. Figure 3-62 displays the default logon page. The user enters a user name and password and then clicks Log On.

FIGURE 3-62

After the user logs on and the portal page appears, the user might notice that there is an icon in the system tray that provides information about the Remote Desktop Client options. When the user right-clicks the icon, three options appear. These are: Open RemoteApp And Desktop Connections, Disconnect All Connections, and Disconnect From Uag.contoso.com, as shown in Figure 3-63.

FIGURE 3-63

The portal page displays the applications that are published through the Forefront UAG server, so in Figure 3-64 you can see the following published applications:

- **Calculator**   A RemoteApp application
- **Paint**   A RemoteApp application
- **Predefined Desktop**   An administrator-defined Remote Desktop Server
- **SharePoint Services**   A Windows SharePoint Services 3.0 server
- **User Chooses RDS Server**   A selection of Remote Desktop Servers to which the user can connect
- **Wordpad**   A RemoteApp application

FIGURE 3-64

Users can click either the large icon in the right pane or the application link in the hierarchical view in the left pane to access the application.

When the user clicks the link for a RemoteApp program, a RemoteApp dialog box appears saying that the Web site is attempting to open the application. Clicking Connect, as seen in Figure 3-65, opens the RemoteApp program.

FIGURE 3-65

The Calculator RemoteApp program appears to a user exactly as a locally installed Calculator application appears. The only way a user would know that the application is not locally installed is by clicking the Help, About menu option. In that case, the Windows Server 2008 R2 banner, rather than the Windows 7 banner, appears, as seen in Figure 3-66.

FIGURE 3-66

When the user clicks the link for a user-defined desktop, a Select Remote Desktop Host dialog box appears, as shown in Figure 3-67. The user enters the name of the RD Session Host server in the Select Remote Desktop Host box and is connected to the specified remote desktop.

FIGURE 3-67

When the user clicks on the SharePoint Server link, the SharePoint site appears in the right pane of the console, as shown in Figure 3-68. The double arrow at the top of the left pane can be used to collapse the left pane to provide more focus on the SharePoint site.

FIGURE 3-68

When a user clicks the link for the administrator-defined desktop, a warning that the Web site is trying to open the RemoteApp program appears. The user then clicks Connect to enable the connection, as shown in Figure 3-69.

FIGURE 3-69

A Windows Security dialog box appears, as shown in Figure 3-70. This lets the user log on to the RD Session Host server, after which access to the site is enabled.

FIGURE 3-70

Administrator's Punch List

In this chapter you were introduced to the Forefront UAG method of publishing applications using portals. Portal trunks can be HTTP or HTTPS. If you choose to publish secure HTTPS portals, you will need to have a Web site certificate that includes the private key installed on the Forefront UAG server. After you create the portal, you can publish applications within it. Forefront UAG includes a number of wizards that make it easy to publish many of today's popular network applications, including Exchange Web services, SharePoint, and Remote Desktop Gateway services.

Key takeaways from this chapter that will help you publish your applications successfully the first time you try include:

- All applications must be published using a portal.
- You can create either HTTP or HTTPS portal trunks.
- Forefront UAG supports a wide variety of authentication providers.
- You can use wildcard and SAN certificates for HTTPS trunks.
- You can use the built-in endpoint detection included with Forefront UAG or you can use an existing NAP infrastructure for endpoint detection when users connect to the portal.
- You can publish OWA, ActiveSync, and RPC/HTTP applications through a Forefront UAG portal.
- A Forefront UAG server or array can host Remote Desktop Gateway services.
- You can publish entire desktops or RemoteApp programs using the Forefront UAG RD Gateway services.
- You can publish administrator-controlled desktops that force specific configuration parameters to be met before users are given access.

CHAPTER 4

Implementing SSL VPN with Forefront UAG

- Understanding SSL VPN Options **95**

- Planning and Configuring SSTP **96**

- Configuring SSL Network Tunneling **102**

E nabling a user to securely access corporate resources from anywhere is one of the goals of Microsoft Forefront Unified Access Gateway (UAG) 2010. One of the biggest challenges in reaching this goal is to make connecting to local resources while a user is at a remote location as transparent as possible, even when the user is located on a network that might otherwise block access attempts to access desired network resources. Virtual Private Networking (VPN) is a core solution for this scenario, but many of the traditional VPN protocols include barriers that prevent seamless access from any location. With a Secure Sockets Layer (SSL) VPN, the remote access experience moves to another level and provides a better experience for the end user. This chapter will describe the way Forefront UAG implements SSL VPN using Secure Socket Tunneling Protocol (SSTP) and Network Tunneling.

Understanding SSL VPN Options

Forefront UAG inherits the core SSL VPN functionality provided by SSL Network Tunneling from its predecessor, Intelligent Application Gateway (IAG). The new feature in Forefront UAG is the SSTP capability. From the end user's perspective, the main difference between these methods is that when using SSTP, you do not need to connect to the portal to establish the SSL VPN connection. You can use the VPN client that is built into Windows Vista (or higher) and choose SSTP as the protocol for the VPN connection, as shown in Figure 4-1.

FIGURE 4-1

The only caveat when using SSTP is that it requires that Forefront UAG be part of the domain. Another option for SSL VPN is to use the SSL Network Tunneling that was inherited from IAG, which uses the Forefront UAG network connector to establish the VPN tunnel. However, there remain many advantages to using the new capability provided by SSTP, including:

- No driver installation needs to be done on the remote client.
- There is no need to launch a portal and then connect to the network connector.
- SSTP supports the use of the internal Dynamic Host Configuration Protocol (DHCP) server rather than the Network Connector, which only supports static pool.

Planning and Configuring SSTP

Some work needs to be done before SSTP can be implemented on Forefront UAG. Most of this work is related to the way the client will access the SSTP VPN, the name it will use, the certificate it will use, and who will issue the certificate. Planning the certificate for SSTP is a key step, and not planning the certificate up front can cause many problems during the operations phase. For this example, we will use the topology shown in Figure 4-2.

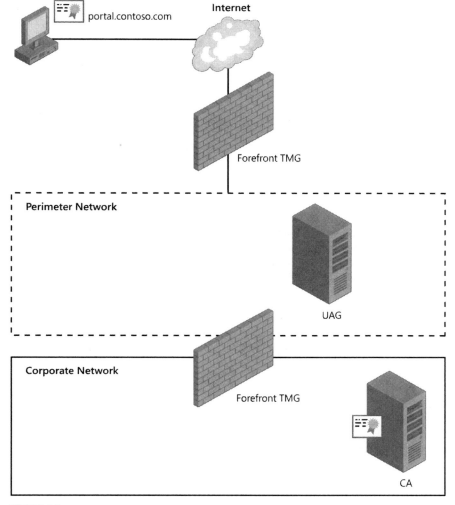

FIGURE 4-2

This topology shows that Forefront UAG is placed in a perimeter network between two Forefront TMG firewalls. Client workstations connect using the name "portal.contoso.com," and the certificate used by the client was issued by an internal certificate authority (CA), located behind the second TMG firewall, within the internal corporate network. Understanding the topology is important so that you understand the traffic flow.

The following items need to be addressed before SSTP can be configured:

- A portal trunk needs to be created on Forefront UAG.
- The client workstation needs to trust the root CA that issued the certificate that will be used for the SSTP connection. If this is not correctly implemented, when the client tries to connect, the error message shown in Figure 4-3 appears.

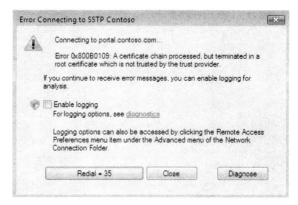

FIGURE 4-3

- The client workstation needs to be able to locate the certificate revocation list (CRL), which is stamped on the certificate, as shown in Figure 4-4.

FIGURE 4-4

- If the client is unable to connect to the CRL, the client workstation displays the error shown in Figure 4-5.

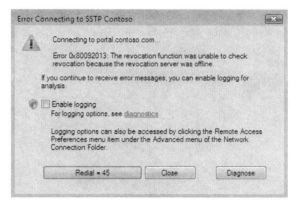

FIGURE 4-5

NOTE For more information on troubleshooting SSTP error codes, read the article "How to debug SSTP specific connection failures," at *http://blogs.technet.com/rrasblog/archive /2007/09/26/how-to-debug-sstp-specific-connection-failures.aspx.*

To mitigate the certificate trust issue, shown in Figure 4-3, you need to import the root CA certificate (.cer file) into the Trusted Root Certification Authorities container within the local computer certificate store. To mitigate the inability to connect to the CRL, shown in Figure 4-5, the CRL needs to be made available to the client workstation. In this particular scenario, this is done by publishing the CRL (via HTTP) on the Forefront TMG that is located in front of the Forefront UAG Server. The public name for this publishing rule needs to match the name shown in Figure 4-4.

For troubleshooting purposes, you can disable CRL checking on the client workstation by adding the registry key HKLM\System\CurrentControlSet\Services\Sstpsvc\parameters \ NoCertRevocationCheck (type DWORD) to 1.

IMPORTANT This is not a fix for the problem. It should be used only when troubleshooting, to isolate whether the issue is on the certificate or on a Forefront UAG configuration. Once you isolate and fix the root cause of the problem, you should either delete this registry key or change it to 0.

Configuring SSTP on Forefront UAG

To configure the SSTP VPN, open the Forefront UAG Management console and complete the following steps:

1. Click the Admin menu, select Remote Network Access, and click SSL Network Tunneling (SSTP). When the SSL Network Tunnel Configuration appears, select the Enable Remote

Client VPN Access checkbox, and choose the Trunk (portal.contoso.com in this example), and then, for this example, change the Maximum VPN Client Connection to 20, as shown in Figure 4-6.

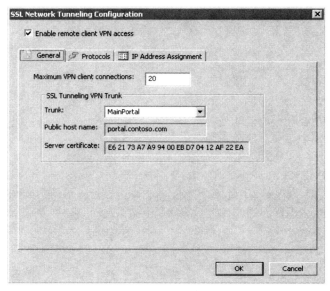

FIGURE 4-6

2. Click the Protocols tab, and ensure that only Secure Socket Tunneling Protocol (SSTP) is selected, as shown in Figure 4-7.

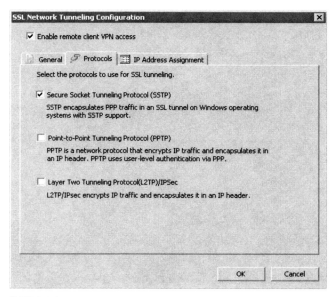

FIGURE 4-7

3. Click the IP Address Assignment tab, and ensure that the Assign Address Using DHCP option is selected, as shown in Figure 4-8.

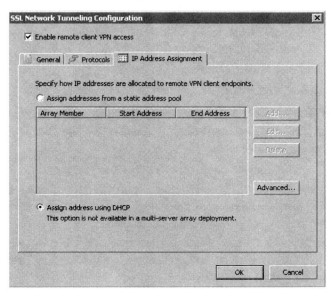

FIGURE 4-8

4. Click Advanced, and ensure that both Obtain DNS Server Addresses Using DHCP and Obtain WINS Server Addresses Using DHCP are selected, as shown in Figure 4-9.

FIGURE 4-9

5. Click OK, click OK again, and activate the configuration by choosing Activate in the File menu.

Client Experience with SSTP

After you finish the SSTP configuration on Forefront UAG, you need to create a VPN Dial Up interface on the remote client workstation and choose the SSTP option. From a client workstation (in this example using Windows Vista), complete the following steps to create your connection and access the SSL VPN using SSTP:

1. Click Start, Network, and click Network And Sharing Center.
2. In the Network And Sharing Center window, click Set Up A Connection Or Network.
3. Choose the option to Connect To A Workplace and click Next.
4. On the Do You Want To Use A Connection That You Already Have page, click No, Create A New Connection, and click Next.
5. On the How Do You Want To Connect page, click Use My Internet Connection (VPN).
6. On the Type The Internet Address To Connect To page, type the address of the SSTP server; in this case, type **portal.contoso.com**. Then type a descriptive name for the connection, and click Next.
7. On the Type Your User Name And Password page, type the name of the user who will use this connection, that user's password, and the domain name, then click Create to create the VPN connection, followed by Close.
8. Return to the Network And Sharing Center and click Change Adapter Settings.
9. Right-click the VPN connection that you just created, and choose Properties.
10. On the Security tab, click the Type Of VPN drop-down list, and select Secure Socket Tunneling Protocol (SSTP), as shown earlier in Figure 4-1.
11. Click OK to finish.

The connection is ready to use. Notice that the client experience in this case is the same as it is for the traditional PPTP or LT2P connection using a VPN client on Windows.

> **NOTE** For more help deploying the SSTP Dial Up connection for users, you can use the "Connection Manager Administration Kit (CMAK)," at *http://technet.microsoft.com/en-us/library/cc753977(WS.10).aspx.*

Configuring SSL Network Tunneling

Another way to connect clients to the internal network using SSL VPN technology is by using SSL network tunneling with Network Connector. When using this option, the user must access the portal first, perform the logon, and then launch the network connector to be fully connected via SSL VPN. The topology that will be used for this example is shown in Figure 4-2. The core requirements for implementing SSL VPN on Contoso's network are:

- Clients should be able to connect to internal resources and be assigned an IP address that is valid on the internal network.

- Regular Internet traffic originating from the remote client will not be handled by a corporate resource (split tunneling is enabled).

- Each client workstation should have access to the main headquarters network (10.20.20.0/24) and to one branch office network (10.30.30.0/24). The networks behind the headquarters network should not be accessed by SSL VPN clients.

- During the initial deployment phase, only users who are members of the Domain Admins group should have access to the Network Connector through the portal.

To enable this scenario, open the Forefront UAG Management console and configure the Network Connector by completing the following steps:

1. In the Admin menu, select Remote Network Access, and click SSL Network Tunneling.

2. On the SSL Network Tunneling Server page, select the Activate SSL Network Tunneling option. In the Use The Following Connection drop-down list, select the Internal network, as shown in Figure 4-10. In the Gateway box under the Complimentary Data section, type the IP address of the default gateway that will be used by the VPN clients.

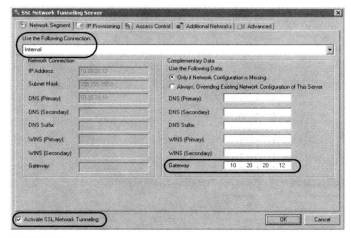

FIGURE 4-10

> *NOTE* **The IP address for the default gateway will vary according to your network topology.**

3. Click the IP Provisioning tab. For this example, be sure that the Corporate IP Addresses option is selected, so that VPN clients can use the same range that the internal network uses (this was one of Contoso's four core requirements for this scenario), as shown in Figure 4-11.

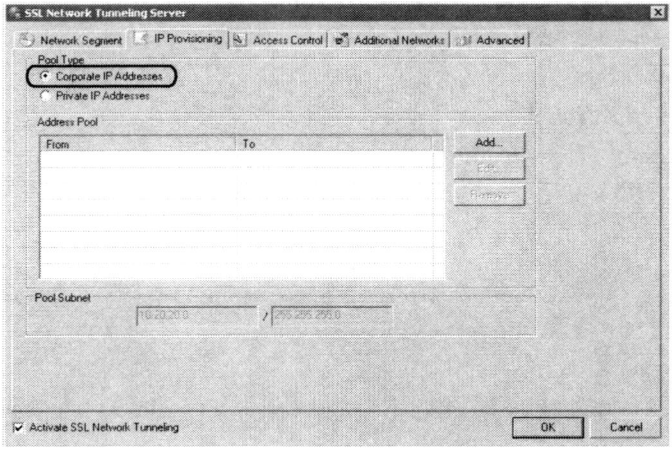

FIGURE 4-11

> **NOTE** Network Connector doesn't support the use of the internal DHCP Server to provide IP addresses for SSL VPN clients, as SSTP does.

4. Click Add to add the IP range that will be used by SSL VPN Clients. Be sure to exclude the IP range from the internal DHCP Server, otherwise you can cause IP conflicts. For this particular example, type the IP range From **10.20.20.135** To **10.20.20.145**. Click OK.

5. Click the Access Control tab, and select the option Split Tunneling (Route Internet Traffic Through Original Client Connection), which is a requirement for this configuration, as shown in Figure 4-12.

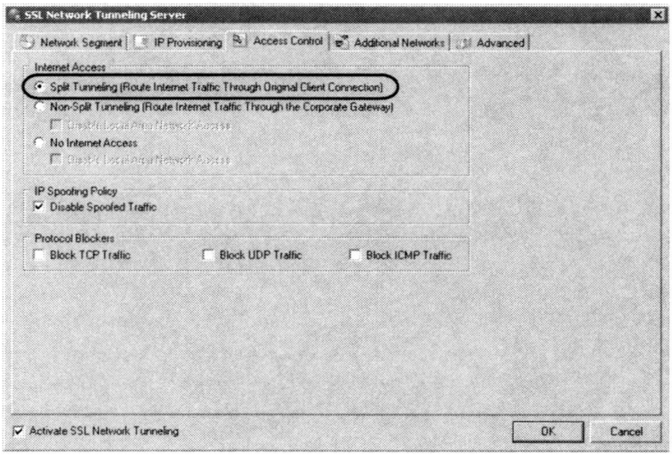

FIGURE 4-12

This tab has these additional options:

- **Non-Split Tunneling (Route Internet Traffic Through The Corporate Gateway)** Choose this option when you want to route all Internet traffic that originates from the VPN client through Forefront UAG, to the company's gateway, and then to the Internet.

- **No Internet Access** This option blocks the VPN Client from having any Internet access.

- **IP Spoofing Policy** This option allows Forefront UAG to analyze the traffic and determine whether the traffic coming in is considered to be spoofed. If the Disable Spoofed Traffic option is enabled, Forefront UAG will drop the packet that is considered to be spoofed.

- **Protocol Blockers** Use this option to block TCP traffic (which blocks all TCP traffic), UDP Traffic (which blocks all UDP traffic), or ICMP traffic (which blocks all ICMP traffic).

6. Click the Additional Networks tab and select the Enable Access To The Following Additional Networks checkbox, as shown in Figure 4-13.

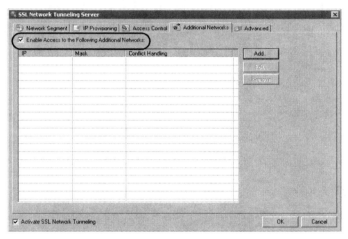

FIGURE 4-13

7. Click Add, and type the IP address range for the network to which you want to allow access, as shown in Figure 4-14.

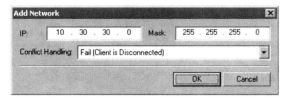

FIGURE 4-14

The default Conflict Handling option, shown in Figure 4-14, is Fail (Client Is Disconnected), which means that if the local network settings for the VPN client conflict with the settings for the network (in this case 10.30.30.0/24) to which the client is trying to connect, the client will be disconnected.

The other options are:

- **Prompt (User Selection)** The user will be prompted to select a preference to either fail the connection or skip access to this network.

- **Skip (Don't Add This Network)** Access to this network will not succeed; the client will stay connected but won't have access to the conflicted network (in this case 10.30.30.0/24).

Click OK to close this window.

8. Click the Advanced tab, and leave the default values selected, as shown in Figure 4-15.

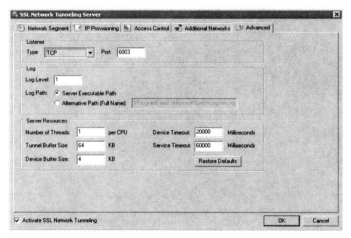

FIGURE 4-15

The following options are available on the Advanced tab:

- **Listener** Allows you to select the type of protocol (in this case, TCP) and the port (default is 6003). This port will be used later when publishing the Network Connector through the trunk portal.

- **Log** You can choose the log level (1 to 5, where 5 is the most verbose) and the location in which you want to store the log.

- **Server Resources** This option allows you to change the default settings for the server resources. Those options should not be changed without proper guidance from a Microsoft representative.

9. Click OK to conclude this part of the configuration. A pop-up window appears inform-
   ing you about the IP exclusion, as shown in Figure 4-16. The message below appears
   with the addresses 10.20.20.143 and 10.20.20.145 because Forefront UAG will not
   allocate those IP addresses to VPN clients. Click OK to continue.

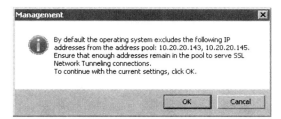

FIGURE 4-16

10. From the File menu, select Activate, and then click Activate.

11. On the Main Portal trunk, under Applications, click Add.

12. On the Welcome To The Add Application Wizard page, click Next to continue.

13. On the Step 1 – Select Application page, select Client/Server And Legacy option, and
    change the drop-down selection to Remote Network Access, as shown in Figure 4-17.
    Click Next to continue.

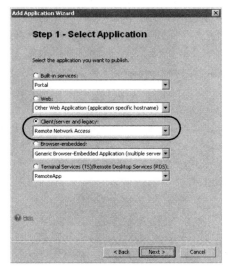

FIGURE 4-17

14. On the Step 2 – Configure Application page, type the name for the application. In this
    case, type **Network Connector**, as shown in Figure 4-18. Click Next to continue.

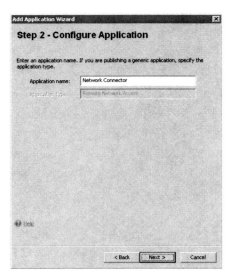

FIGURE 4-18

15. On the Step 3 – Select Endpoint Policies page, leave the default policy selected, and click Next.

16. On the Step 4 – Configure Server Settings page, be sure to use the default options, as shown in Figure 4-19. Notice that the port suggested by the Wizard is the same port that was used during the Network Connector configuration, and that the Server field corresponds to the loopback address (127.0.0.1). Click Next to proceed.

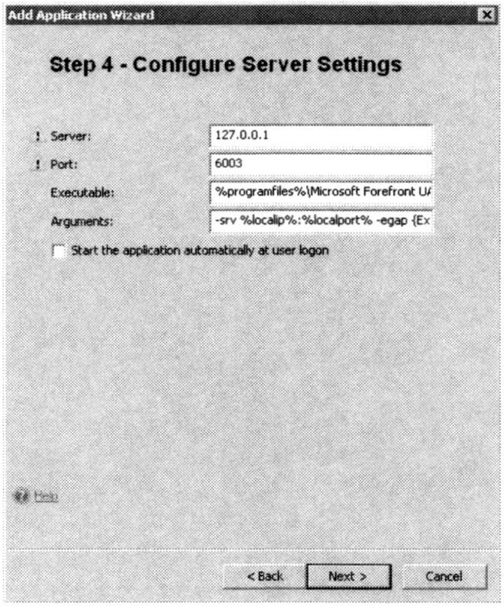

FIGURE 4-19

17. On the Step 5 – Portal Link page, review the name that will appear in the portal. By default, Forefront UAG uses the name that was specified in Step 2. Leave the other options set to the defaults, and click Next to continue.

18. On the Step 6 – Authorization page you have the opportunity to identify the users or groups that will have access to the Network Connector. Contoso's network requirements state that only members of the Domain Admins group should have access to the Network Connector. In order to comply with that requirement, uncheck the Authorize All Users option, then click Add. In the Look In drop-down list, select the authentication repository Active Directory, double-click the Users folder, select Domain Admins, click Add, and then click OK. At this point, your Authorization page should match Figure 4-20. Click Next to proceed.

FIGURE 4-20

19. On the Completing The Add Application Wizard page, click Finish.

20. Activate your configuration by choosing Activate in the File menu.

Customizing Network Connector Settings

After you finish configuring the Network Connector application within the portal the application is ready to be used. However, there are certain scenarios in which you might need to change some settings that are not available through the wizard. If that is the case, you can open the settings for this application to customize them. To access the properties of the Network Connector that you created in the previous step, under Applications, click Edit.

In the Main Portal trunk, under Applications, select the application and click Edit. This will open Application Properties (Remote Network Access). Many options are the same as the options that were configured through the wizard, but it is important to look at the Client Settings tab, as shown in Figure 4-21.

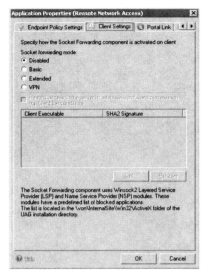

FIGURE 4-21

As the description at the bottom of the window says, the socket forwarding component on Forefront UAG is composed of two core components: Winsock2 Layered Service Provider (LSP) and Name Service Provider (NSP). These components will intercept all network traffic passing through Forefront UAG from the client. This should be a transparent process for the applications. When the client workstation that connects using Network Connector tries to access a resource, the Windows operating system will load the NSP module if the application is performing a name resolution, and it will load the LSP module if the application is using sockets to connect to a remote server.

> **NOTE** For more information about the Winsock 2 LSP and NSP architecture, read "Unraveling the Mysteries of Writing a Winsock 2 Layered Service Provider," at *http://www.microsoft.com/msj/0599/LayeredService/LayeredService.aspx.*

Although the process of using socket forwarding should be transparent from the application's perspective, there is a chance that the application won't behave correctly when it is integrated with this component, so this option is disabled by default. The other available options for forwarding mode are:

- **Basic**   When this mode is selected, none of the applications that eventually load the Socket Forwarding components (LSP or NSP modules) can access corporate resources, unless the Forefront UAG SSL Application Tunneling component is running on the client workstation and at least one tunnel is open. From the security standpoint, this mode blocks all Windows services (non-interactive applications) from accessing configured corporate resources, regardless of the status of the SSL Application Tunneling component.

- **Extended** If this mode is enabled, the same settings that Basic mode uses will be used, except that Windows services will be allowed to access configured corporate resources.

- **VPN** When this mode is enabled, the LSP and NSP components are always active in all applications. This means that access to configured corporate resources is enabled, with exceptions for applications that are in the block list.

For the purpose of this example, leave the default options selected and click OK.

Client Experience with Network Connector

The client experience with Network Connector is different from the experience of connecting through the VPN using SSTP Dial-Up Client. In this particular case, the access to the portal is mandatory: Without accessing the portal you can't launch Network Connector (at least, you can't launch it in a supported manner). To verify the client's experience and also validate your implementation, connect to the portal using the FQDN you designated for the portal trunk, and verify that you now have an icon for the Network Connector, as shown in Figure 4-22.

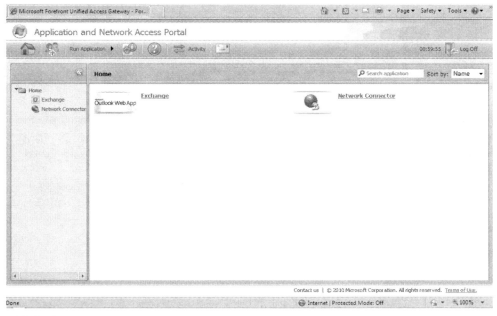

FIGURE 4-22

When you launch Network Connector for the first time, you will notice that the components will be downloaded to the local client workstation, as shown in Figure 4-23.

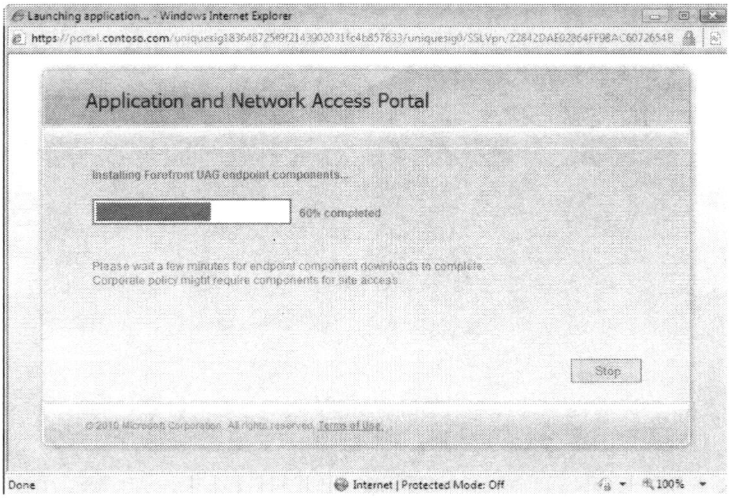

FIGURE 4-23

Once the components are installed and the Network Connector establishes the SSL connection with Forefront UAG, a balloon notifying you that the connection has started appears in the lower right corner of your window, as shown in Figure 4-24.

FIGURE 4-24

At this point, the user is connected, has already received an internal IP address (from the specified pool range), and should be able to access corporate network resources. To verify the current status of the connection, click the Activity button on the portal, and the Portal Activity dialog box appears, as shown in Figure 4-25.

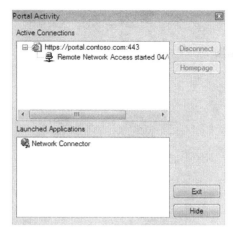

FIGURE 4-25

NOTE Don't click Exit to close the window unless you want to close the connection. Exit causes the Network Connector to close the connection. Click the Hide button to close the window but stay connected.

Administrator's Punch List

- Plan your SSL VPN deployment before you start to configure it.
- Determine the option that is best for your company: SSTP or Network Connector.
- Be sure to identify the certificate that will be used by the SSTP connection.
- Be sure that the client workstations trust the CA and have access to the CRL.
- Use CMAK to deploy the SSTP Dial-Up connection for SSTP VPN users.
- When using Network Connector, remember that the use of internal DHCP is not supported.
- Evaluate your application to determine whether it is necessary to make adjustments to Socket Forwarding.
- Educate users so they understand how to use the Network Connector, and remind them that if they close the portal the Network Connector will also close.

CHAPTER 5

Implementing Forefront UAG with DirectAccess

- How DirectAccess Works **116**

- Forefront UAG 2010 DirectAccess Requirements **141**

- Forefront UAG 2010 DirectAccess Configuration Wizard **142**

DirectAccess is a new remote access technology, enabled by Windows 7 and Windows Server 2008 R2, that allows users to be connected to the corporate network at all times. From your users' points of view, the computer experience is the same regardless of their locations. Users can move from the corporate network to Internet cafés, to hotel rooms, to conference centers, and even to airplanes, and, as long as they are connected to the Internet, they will be able to reach resources on the corporate network as if they were directly connected to it via an Ethernet connection or 802.11 wireless link.

Users never need to open a VPN connection and they don't need to remember the URL for an SSL VPN gateway (even if that SSL VPN gateway is a Forefront UAG server). They don't need to do anything; they just click links in their emails or on their desktops or type in the server names they always use, and then they connect.

At first, this always-on aspect might seem like the most compelling component of the DirectAccess solution. However, DirectAccess offers even more than transparent connectivity to your users. Because the DirectAccess connection is a bidirectional link, you always have the ability to connect to the DirectAccess clients on the Internet. Whenever the DirectAccess client computer is turned on (your users don't even need to log on in order for you to connect to DirectAccess clients from within your corporate network), you can connect and manage the DirectAccess client. This means that the management infrastructure that you use now to control and configure hosts on the corporate network continues to operate for client computers that are connected via DirectAccess.

In fact, from our work so far with a number of enterprise administrators who have deployed DirectAccess, it appears that this ability to "manage out" (remotely manage) DirectAccess clients is even more compelling than the transparent connectivity users have to resources on the corporate network. These enterprise administrators consider the always-on connectivity interesting, but they really get excited by the idea that they will always be able to manage the DirectAccess clients using Group Policy and other systems management tools. The inability to manage remote clients appears to be a real problem for many enterprises: Employees are given corporate laptops, and they might occasionally connect over a VPN connection, but, most often, these users don't return to the corporate network for months, years, or sometimes ever again. The result is always that these machines slowly but surely fall out of compliance and become increasingly susceptible to malware and other types of compromise. System stability issues even slip in, and those end up decreasing employee productivity and increasing costs for help desk use.

This chapter discusses some of the technologies that are used to make DirectAccess work and provides information about the network infrastructure components needed as part of a DirectAccess solution. The chapter ends with a step-by-step description of the Forefront UAG DirectAccess Wizard.

How DirectAccess Works

DirectAccess brings to bear a number of technologies that are part of the Windows 7 and Windows Server 2008 R2 platforms. Some of these technologies are new, and some you have been using for a long time. However, whether you're working with old or new technologies, none of them needs to be prohibitively complex. It's important to keep this in mind, because you might have read in other places that DirectAccess might not be worth the effort due to the level of complexity involved.

This reputation might come from the fact that, before Forefront UAG 2010 was released, the only way you could deploy DirectAccess was by using the built-in Windows DirectAccess solution. Although the Windows DirectAccess solution does work, Forefront UAG DirectAccess adds to the core Windows implementation to make DirectAccess enterprise–ready:

- Windows DirectAccess has limited support for high availability, and the mechanism recommended involves using Hyper-V and Windows failover clustering. There is no support for Network Load Balancing.

- Windows DirectAccess does not support DirectAccess arrays. If you want to deploy multiple Windows DirectAccess servers, you need to configure and manage them individually. In contrast, Forefront UAG DirectAccess servers can be configured in arrays of up to eight.

- Windows DirectAccess servers do not support IPv4-only servers. DirectAccess clients on the Internet will not be able to connect to IPv4-only servers. That means that if you want to use the Windows DirectAccess solution, you need to upgrade your servers to Windows Server 2008 or above. In contrast, the Forefront UAG DirectAccess solution fully supports IPv4-only servers on the corporate network.

If you plan to deploy DirectAccess on your enterprise network, you need to use the Forefront UAG DirectAccess solution.

DirectAccess Client Connectivity

IPv6 is the core of the DirectAccess solution, which is one of the reasons why many admin-istrators feel like they can't deploy it at this time. IPv6 has the potential to be complex, and, with your IT group and budget shrinking, you might not have the time to devote to learning an entirely new networking protocol. The good news is that you don't need to become an IPv6 expert to make DirectAccess work for you and your company, because the Forefront UAG DirectAccess solution automatically deploys the IPv6 infrastructure you need to get started.

When the DirectAccess client is on the Internet, it will try to establish two IPsec tunnels to the Forefront UAG DirectAccess server. These tunnels use IPsec tunnel mode and the Encapsulating Security Payload (ESP) protocol with AES 192-bit encryption for privacy over the Internet.

The names of these tunnels are:

- **Infrastructure tunnel**   The infrastructure tunnel starts up when the computer starts but before the user logs on. The DirectAccess computer is always a domain member and the computer account is used to log on via computer certificate and NTLMv2 authentication. In addition, the computer must belong to a security group that is dedi-cated to DirectAccess client computers. This tunnel is bidirectional, so management agents on the client can call in to management servers on the corporate network, and your IT management servers can initiate connections to the DirectAccess clients while the infrastructure tunnel is up. The DirectAccess client can connect only to servers that you stipulate through the infrastructure tunnel; the infrastructure tunnel does not allow open access to the entire corporate network.

- **Intranet tunnel**   The intranet tunnel is established after the user logs on. This tunnel is also encrypted using ESP and AES 192. Tunnel authentication is performed using a computer certificate (the same certificate as that used by the infrastructure tunnel) and Kerberos authentication for the user account. The intranet tunnel allows the user to access any resource on the corporate network for which that user is authorized.

There are two access models that you can use when enabling DirectAccess clients to con-nect to the corporate network:

- **End-to-Edge**   When you use the end-to-edge connection model, the DirectAccess clients establish an authenticated IPsec tunnel mode link to the Forefront UAG DirectAccess server. After terminating the IPsec connection at the DirectAccess server, the traffic moving from the DirectAccess server to servers on the corporate network is neither authenticated nor encrypted at the network level.

- **End-to-End**   The end-to-end network security model enables you to secure connec-tions with IPsec from the DirectAccess client to a host inside your corporate network. The connection between the DirectAccess client and server is encrypted and authenti-cated using IPsec tunnel mode. When traffic leaves the DirectAccess server to go to a server on the corporate network, the connection between the client and the server is passed over the corporate network, using IPsec transport mode. However, the default setting is for authentication to the endpoint only; the transport mode connection is not encrypted so that network IDS and other security devices can evaluate the connections over the network. This also reduces some of the processing overhead involved with IPsec connectivity.

In addition to the computer certificate, computer account (NTLMv2), and user account (Kerberos) authentication used in creating the DirectAccess tunnels, you also have the option to force users to use smart card authentication to establish the intranet tunnel, further enhancing the overall security of the solution. And, if smart card authentication is not enough, you can enforce endpoint detection and enforcement on the DirectAccess client using NAP, so that non-compliant computers are quarantined and remediated before the intranet tunnel can be established.

It is important to note that end-to-edge connectivity supports all networks, so you don't need to have any IPv6-ready hosts on the corporate network to support end-to-edge scenarios. However, if you want to deploy end-to-end security with IPsec transport mode, the servers behind the DirectAccess server will need to be using Windows Server 2008 or above and be IPv6-capable. In addition, you can mix end-to-edge and end-to-end connectivity models because they are not mutually exclusive.

All traffic moving between the DirectAccess client and server is IPv6 traffic. This will always be the case. The implication of this is that while the servers behind the Forefront UAG DirectAccess server don't need to be IPv6-capable, the client application must always be IPv6-aware. For this reason, you'll need to be sure you qualify your client applications to make sure they're IPv6-compatible before you fully deploy the DirectAccess solution.

Admin Insight

You might have noticed that terms such as "IPv6-aware," "IPv6-capable," "IPv6-only," and "native-IPv6" have been used, but not defined. This is something that you'll encounter with the public documentation of DirectAccess, and it can be somewhat confusing to someone who's new to the IPv6 space. When referring to "native IPv6" networks, there is the assumption that all network infrastructure (routers, DNS, DHCP, and so on), clients, and servers are using a full-blown IPv6 deployment. In contrast, an "IPv6-aware" deployment isn't using IPv6 from end to end, but client and server applications can take advantage of IPv6 transition technologies to work on IPv4 networks. The "IPv6-capable" network has hosts on it that support the Intra-Site Automatic Tunnel Addressing Protocol (ISATAP) so that IPv6 messages can be sent over an IPv4 network. When you install Forefront UAG as your DirectAccess server, it will configure itself as an ISATAP router, so that IPv6 messages can be tunneled within an IPv4 header over your IPv4 network, and you won't need to upgrade your routers and switches or DNS and DHCP servers to work with IPv6 connectivity.

IPv6 Transition Technologies

Most of us live in an IPv4 world, and it's likely that we're going to live in that world for a long time. While there are some cutting edge networks that are moving toward IPv6, even those with government mandates to move to IPv6 have been slow at deploying it and haven't fully moved. In addition, there are very few computers that have access to the IPv6 Internet, and the time it takes the Internet to move to IPv6 could be even longer than the time private networks take.

Because the DirectAccess client uses IPv6 to connect to the DirectAccess server and possibly to other servers on the corporate network, there must be a method you can use to allow these IPv6 messages to move over an IPv4 Internet and IPv4 intranets. DirectAccess solves these problems by using a number of transition technologies that allow IPv6 messages to be tunneled in IPv4 headers. These are:

- **The Intra-Site Automatic Tunnel Addressing Protocol (ISATAP)**   ISATAP is used on intranets so that ISATAP-capable hosts can use IPv6 to communicate with one another. ISATAP hosts do this by instantiating an ISATAP tunnel adapter that has an IPv6 address bound to it, and then the ISATAP host wraps these ISATAP communications inside an IPv4 header so that they can be sent over the intranet routing infrastructure. When the communication reaches its destination server, the IPv4 header is removed and the IPv6 header and payload is exposed. ISATAP allows you to take full advantage of IPv6 communications without requiring you to upgrade your network gear and routing infrastructure to support IPv6.

- **The 6to4 Protocol**   The 6to4 protocol is used by the DirectAccess client when the DirectAccess client is assigned a public IP address. Similarly to the way the ISATAP adapter works, a 6to4 tunnel adapter is automatically configured on the DirectAccess client, which has an IPv6 address bound to it. The DirectAccess client's IPv6 communications sent out by this adapter are encapsulated with an IPv4 header so that they can traverse the IPv4-only Internet to the DirectAccess server. The Forefront UAG DirectAccess Wizard automatically configures the Forefront UAG DirectAccess server as a 6to4 router for your organization. You don't need to know anything about 6to4, if you are not interested in it, except for the fact that 6to4 requires that all interposed devices between the DirectAccess client and server allow IP protocol 41 inbound and outbound.

- **The Teredo Protocol**   The Teredo protocol is another IPv6 transition technology that the DirectAccess client can use to connect to the Forefront UAG DirectAccess server over an IPv4 Internet. Teredo is used when the DirectAccess client is assigned a private IP address, but has outbound access to UDP port 3544 on the Forefront UAG DirectAccess server. With Teredo, the IPv6 communications are sent through the Teredo adapter that is automatically configured on the DirectAccess client. The IPv6 message is encapsulated with an IPv4 header, which is then encapsulated with a UDP header. Teredo is the reason that two public IP addresses must be assigned to the external interface of the Forefront UAG DirectAccess server and also the reason you need to allow ICMPv6 echo requests to intranet servers with which you want the DirectAccess client to communicate. Those two addresses are used to determine behind which type of Network Address Translation (NAT) device the DirectAccess client is located. In addition, all devices need to enable ping in order for the Teredo client to connect to them.

- **The IP-HTTPS Protocol** IP-HTTPS is an entirely new protocol developed by Microsoft to allow DirectAccess clients to connect to the UAG DirectAccess server when only outbound TCP port 443 is allowed. You'll see this when there are port-restricted firewalls set up in front of the DirectAccess client or when the organization in which the DirectAccess client is located allows outbound access only through a Web proxy device. With IP-HTTPS, the DirectAccess client starts up an IP-HTTPS tunnel adapter and sends its messages over that. The IPv6 messages are encapsulated in an IPv4 header, which is then encapsulated in an HTTP header. The HTTP header is then encrypted using SSL (TLS) encryption. As you can imagine, there is significantly higher protocol overhead and high processing overhead (due to the IPsec encryption and the HTTPS encryption), so performance for an IP-HTTPS connection is likely to suffer. Even if you use modern server processors (such as the Intel 5300 series, which includes AES-NI technology on the chip) that can offload much of the encryption processing, you still have to deal with the protocol overhead, so it ends up taking more packets to send the same amount of data. In addition, when the DirectAccess client is located behind a Web proxy server, the Web proxy server cannot require authentication for outbound access, because the DirectAccess client doesn't have a provision for entering authentication information that can be used by the Web proxy server. Also, your users will need to configure the IP-HTTPS adapter to use the Web proxy server by initiating a netsh command, so that the IP-HTTPS client knows what Web proxy server to use.

It should be clear, at this point, that you want to avoid the IP-HTTPS configuration if you can. The DirectAccess client, when assigned a private IP address, will try to use Teredo, which provides reasonably good performance. Only when Teredo isn't available will the DirectAccess client fall back to using IP-HTTPS.

While it might seem as though all these IPv6 transition technologies are a lot to take in, remember that the Forefront UAG DirectAccess Wizard does all the work for you. It configures the Forefront UAG DirectAccess server as a 6to4 router, as a Teredo relay and router, and as an IP-HTTPS gateway. You don't need to have a deep (or even moderate) understanding of these protocols to get DirectAccess working; all this IPv6 technology works behind the scenes to allow seamless and transparent connectivity for your DirectAccess clients.

Admin Insight

I n work we've done with a number of enterprise IT departments who are deploying DirectAccess to 1,000 or more clients, the distribution of DirectAccess client connections appears to be around 70 percent Teredo, 30 percent IP-HTTPS, and 5 percent 6to4. However, this distribution might change depending on how popular the requirement for disabling split tunneling becomes.

The Name Resolution Policy Table (NRPT)

The Name Resolution Policy Table (NRPT) is used by the DirectAccess client to determine which DNS servers it should use, depending on the domain name or FQDN of the destination to which it's trying to connect. With the help of the NRPT, your DirectAccess clients will know to send DNS queries to the Forefront UAG DirectAccess server for name resolution when names within your intranet need to be resolved, and to send DNS queries for names outside your organization to the DNS server address configured on the DirectAccess client's network interface.

For example, suppose the Contoso organization has many subdomains that lie under the contoso.com root domain. These domains can be in the same or different forests; in terms of name resolution, it does not matter. When you configure the NRPT, you set it with an entry that says all requests for domains that match *.contoso.com should be sent to the IPv6 address of the Forefront UAG DirectAccess server. The reason name resolution requests are sent to the IPv6 address of the Forefront UAG DirectAccess server is that Forefront UAG takes the place of an intranet DNS server by installing its own DNS proxy (known at the Forefront UAG DNS64 service). The DNS proxy on the Forefront UAG server will use the DNS servers configured on the Forefront UAG DirectAccess server's internal interface to resolve the names requested by the DirectAccess clients.

What happens to names that aren't included in the NRPT? In this case, the DirectAccess client sends name query requests to the DNS server address configured on its network interface. When the DirectAccess client connects to the network, regardless of whether it's behind a NAT device or assigned a public address, it will receive a DNS server address from a DHCP server. It's this address that the DirectAccess client will use to resolve all names that aren't part of the organization's namespace.

This type of DNS routing (which can be thought of as a method of *conditional DNS forwarding*) gives rise to the default DirectAccess client configuration that enables split tunneling. The reason we chose to make split tunneling the default configuration is that it significantly improves performance for the DirectAccess client. If split tunneling were disabled (which is called force tunneling in DirectAccess parlance), all traffic destined for the corporate network and the Internet would move through the DirectAccess IPsec tunnels.

Some of you might be concerned about split tunneling, because you've been told that split tunneling is bad. While that might have been true for VPN clients in the 1990s, modern Windows operating systems don't enable attackers to route through VPN clients to connect to the corporate network. The situation is even more secure with DirectAccess. Even if an attacker found some way to route connections from the Internet through the DirectAccess client, the connections would fail because IPsec enforces security on the tunnel based on the IPsec connection of the DirectAccess client, in addition to the computer certificate, computer account, user account, and smart card requirements that are needed to establish a connection. Since the security issues that lead to concerns over split tunneling do not and cannot apply to the DirectAccess client, there is no compelling reason to consider split tunneling in a DirectAccess scenario to be a significant security issue.

 SECURITY ALERT We recently discussed the issue of split tunneling with a number of enterprises on an informal basis. Like most experienced network administrators, we were also "believers" that split tunneling, in general, might not be a good idea, and we thought that most enterprise administrators would not allow split tunneling for their VPN clients. We were surprised to find out that over 50 percent of the enterprises that we questioned stated that they now allow their VPN clients to split tunnels, both because the reasons for disabling split tunneling no longer apply and because users became significantly more productive as a result of split tunneling's performance enhancements. If your organization is still prohibiting split tunneling, you might want to review your current policies. In terms of DirectAccess and split tunneling, it's also important to keep in mind that the issues that might have been related to VPN split tunneling are generally not applicable to DirectAccess client /server connections.

The NRPT is also used to prevent the DirectAccess client from resolving specific names, so DNS queries for these names are never sent to the intranet DNS server (which, in the case of Forefront UAG DirectAccess, is the DNS proxy on the Forefront UAG DirectAccess server). The most important example of this is the name of the network location server (NLS). The DirectAccess client uses the NLS to determine whether it's on the corporate network or not. If the DirectAccess client can connect to the NLS, the DirectAccess client knows that it's on the corporate network and it turns off the NRPT. If the DirectAccess client cannot connect to the NLS, then it assumes that it is off the corporate network and leaves the NRPT enabled.

If the NRPT were configured so that the DirectAccess client could resolve the name of the NLS, the DirectAccess client on the Internet would think it was on the corporate network and turn off the NRPT. If the DirectAccess client on the Internet turned off the NRPT, it would not know to send DNS queries for corporate network names to the Forefront UAG DirectAccess server's DNS proxy component, and, therefore, it would never be able to resolve intranet names. To solve this problem, the NRPT is configured with an exception rule that prevents the DirectAccess client on the Internet from resolving the name of the NLS.

For example, if the NRPT is configured to send all queries that match the string *.contoso.com to the DNS64 service on the Forefront UAG DirectAccess server, that would include a query for the name nls.contoso.com, which is the name of the NLS on the corporate network. But, if we create an exception for the name *nls.contoso.com* in the NRPT, even through the name nls.contoso.com matches the string *.contoso.com, the query would not be sent to the DNS proxy on the Forefront UAG DirectAccess server and, instead, would be sent to the DNS server configured on the Forefront UAG DirectAccess client's network interface. Because it wouldn't be able to resolve this name, the DirectAccess client on the Internet will assume that it's off the corporate network, and it will leave the NRPT enabled.

Forefront UAG NAT64/DNS64 and IPv4-Only Corporate Resources

It is likely that most networks you encounter today are a mix of IPv4-only and IPv6-capable clients and servers. It is also likely that there are more IPv4 resources on your network than there are IPv6-capable resources. Given that this is the current networking environment, Forefront UAG DirectAccess needs a way to allow access to IPv4 resources on your network.

Forefront UAG DirectAccess handles the problem by implementing two technologies that are not available in the Windows Server DirectAccess solution:

- NAT64 (pronounced NAT six to four)
- DNS64 (pronounced D-N-S six to four)

These two technologies enable DirectAccess clients, which always speak IPv6 to the Forefront UAG DirectAccess server, to connect to IPv4-only resources on the corporate network.

When a DirectAccess client sends a request for resources using a single label or FQDN, it first consults the NRPT. If there is a match on the NRPT and there is no exception rule for the name, then the DirectAccess client sends the name resolution request to the IP address of the Forefront UAG DirectAccess server. If the request is for a single-label name, then the DirectAccess client's DNS client component will append DNS suffixes as configured on the network interface or through Group Policy.

When the Forefront UAG DirectAccess server receives this request, it sends the request to the DNS servers that are configured on its internal interface in the order in which the DNS servers are listed. The DNS query request will be for both Host (A) and Quad A (AAAA) records. If the DNS server responds to the Forefront UAG DirectAccess server with a Quad A record, it will return this to the DirectAccess client. The DirectAccess client will then connect to the IPv6 address included in the Quad A response over the DirectAccess IPsec tunnels.

However, if the DNS server responds to the Forefront UAG DirectAccess server with only an A record, the DirectAccess client on the Internet is going to have a problem, because the DirectAccess client can only communicate over IPv6. To solve this problem, the Forefront UAG

DirectAccess server's DNS64 component will map the IPv4 address to an IPv6 address, and then it will inform the Forefront UAG DirectAccess server's NAT64 component of the mapping between the IPv6 address and the IPv4 address.

For example, suppose the DirectAccess client on the Internet needs to connect to SRV1. contoso.com. It sends the name query request to the IPv6 address of the Forefront UAG DirectAccess server over the DirectAccess IPsec tunnel. The Forefront UAG DirectAccess server sends an A and an AAAA request for SRV1.contoso.com to the DNS servers configured on its internal interface. The DNS server returns only an A record with the IP address 10.0.0.66. The DNS64 component on the Forefront UAG DirectAccess server maps 10.0.0.66 to an IPv6 address, such as 2002::0066 (this is for example purposes only, this would not be the address actually mapped to this server). The Forefront UAG DirectAccess server's DNS64 component then informs the NAT64 component that the NAT64 component should forward any incoming requests for 2002::0066 to the IPv4 address 10.0.0.66. Session state is also tracked so that responses from 10.0.0.66 are forwarded to the DirectAccess client. The Forefront UAG DirectAccess server forwards the name resolution response for SRV1.contoso.com with the IP address of 2002::0066 to the DirectAccess client on the Internet, and the DirectAccess client sends a connection request to that address.

As you can see, DNS64/NAT64 acts as an IPv6/IPv4 protocol translator, so that the DirectAccess client on the Internet is able to connect to IPv4-only resources on the corporate network. However, in practice, this means that the client-side components installed on the DirectAccess client must be IPv6-aware, but the server-side components do not need to be IPv6-aware. This enormously expands the number of scenarios in which DirectAccess clients can connect to intranet resources.

However, as with all NAT-based solutions, there are some limitations. The primary limitations are:

- NAT64/DNS64 will consume memory and processing resources, so it can have a negative performance impact on the Forefront UAG DirectAccess server.

- NAT64/DNS64 works in a "forward NAT" scenario only. This means that you cannot "reverse NAT" from the corporate network to the DirectAccess client from an IPv4 management station on the intranet, so you will not be able to initiate a connection from an IPv4-only management station to the DirectAccess client. However, the DirectAccess client is able to connect to the management station as long as the DirectAccess client initiates the connection. If your solution can leverage this existing connection, you will be able to connect back to the DirectAccess client.

- NAT64/DNS64 doesn't include any "NAT editors." NAT editors are often used to allow network access over a NAT to applications that embed networking information in their application protocols. For example, the FTP protocol embeds IP addressing information in its protocol, and the OCS client embeds an IPv4 address in its application protocol. These will not work with NAT64/DNS64 because there is no NAT editor to make them work correctly.

These are the primary issues that you might encounter when using the Forefront UAG DirectAccess server's NAT64/DNS64 solution. Keep in mind that NAT64/DNS64 will only be used if the server on which your application is installed doesn't support IPv6 or if the application itself doesn't support IPv6. If the server and application support IPv6, then NAT64/DNS64 won't be used, and the communication from the DirectAccess client to the destination server will be sent to the ISATAP address assigned to the server on the corporate network.

Admin Insight

An interesting fact about Forefront UAG DirectAccess NAT64/DNS64 is that the NAT64 component is part of the TMG application that is installed on the Forefront UAG DirectAccess server, while the DNS64 component is part of the Forefront UAG code.

Infrastructure Components of a Forefront UAG DirectAccess Solution

While the Forefront UAG DirectAccess Wizard does a lot of the configuration for you, there are a number of infrastructure components you need to have in place before you can deploy a Forefront UAG DirectAccess solution. The Forefront UAG DirectAccess Wizard will configure many of these for you, but other components require that you install and configure them separately. The good news is that most of these infrastructure services are ones that you're already using and with which you are already familiar, so the learning curve won't be that steep. The primary challenge that you, as a Forefront UAG DirectAccess administrator, have to deal with is the number of "moving parts" involved in the solution. However, once you have configured Forefront UAG DirectAccess in a lab environment, you'll understand how all of these parts work together, and it will actually end up seeming quite easy to configure.

Admin Insight

We highly recommend that you build out a test lab using Forefront UAG DirectAccess Test Lab Guides. You can find a comprehensive list of Test Lab Guides on the TechNet Wiki at *http://social.technet.microsoft.com/wiki/contents /articles/test-lab-guides.aspx*.

Key components of a Forefront UAG DirectAccess infrastructure include:

- Active Directory Domain Services and Group Policy
- Domain Name Services (DNS)
- A Public Key Infrastructure (PKI) and Windows Active Directory Certificate Services

- Network location servers
- Certificate Revocation List (CRL) servers
- Windows Firewall with Advanced Security and Network Firewalls
- Remote Access VPN servers

The following sections discuss each of these servers and technologies and the ways in which they are integrated into a Forefront UAG DirectAccess solution.

Active Directory Domain Services and Group Policy

Both the DirectAccess client and the Forefront UAG DirectAccess server need to be members of a domain. The DirectAccess client computer account and user login account can be members of different domains or forests from the Forefront UAG DirectAccess server, but in that scenario you need to be sure that there is a two-way trust between the Forefront UAG server forest and the computer/user account forest. There are no provisions for a workgroup configuration on either the client side or the server side.

The reason you need the DirectAccess client and server to be domain members is that Forefront UAG DirectAccess leverages domain Group Policy to deploy many of the parameters of the DirectAccess configuration. For example, the Windows Firewall with Advanced Security is configured on both the DirectAccess clients and Forefront UAG DirectAccess server using Group Policy. Without domain membership, the Group Policy delivery mechanism wouldn't be available. Of course, you could manually configure the Forefront UAG DirectAccess client and server, but this wouldn't be very scalable.

In addition to Group Policy, domain membership enables the ability to map computer certificates in the NTAuth Store in Active Directory. This is required for the computer certificate authentication that is used for authenticating both the first and second IPsec DirectAccess tunnels. If the computer certificate isn't mapped, the computer will not be able to establish these tunnels.

Active Directory also allows us to leverage the ability to automatically deploy certificates via Group Policy. We'll cover computer certificate deployment later, when we discuss PKI and Windows Active Directory Certificate Services.

Another important thing to realize about Active Directory is that there is no specific domain functional level required. You can be running your current Active Directory infrastructure at the Windows Server 2003 functional level and you will still be able to get DirectAccess to work. There is no requirement for a Windows Server 2008 or Windows Server 2008 R2 domain controller.

Domain Name Services (DNS)

DNS is part of all networks, so this won't be a new technology for you. In fact, you can use any version of DNS you like in a Forefront UAG DirectAccess solution. However, the level of functionality you get depends on the servers your DNS version can support. If you want full functionality, your DNS servers should support IPv6 Quad A (AAAA) records and should be able to accept dynamic registrations of these records. If you are using Windows Server 2008 or above as your corporate DNS server, it will meet these requirements.

The IPv6 dynamic registrations are used mostly in two areas:

- IPv6-capable servers on the corporate network will be able to automatically register their native IPv6 or ISATAP addresses with the DNS server, enabling hosts on the corporate network to use IPv6 addresses to communicate with one another.

- Forefront UAG DirectAccess clients on the Internet will register this IPv6 address dynamically, in your DNS database, so that if you want to initiate outbound connections from management stations on the corporate network you can do it using the computer name of the DirectAccess client.

However, you can still use other DNS servers, such as non-Microsoft DNS servers or Windows Server 2003 and below. You might lose some functionality, because these servers might not support dynamic registration of IPv6 records, so DirectAccess clients will need to use NAT64/DNS64 for all of their communications with resources on the corporate network, even if those resources are IPv6-capable. We discussed earlier what some of the limitations of NAT64/DNS64 are, but, if you are comfortable with these limitations, there's no reason that you need to upgrade to Windows Server 2008 or above.

Public Key Infrastructure and Windows Active Directory Certificate Services

In the past, when the subject of a PKI was brought up, many administrators would avoid the topic. However, in the past few years, this reaction seems to have lessened. This is most likely because so many Microsoft servers and services now require certificates, so most administrators have had to learn about PKI to get those services running.

If you don't have any kind of PKI in place, don't let this requirement be a block to your Forefront UAG DirectAccess deployment. The PKI requirements are relatively simple; you need certificates in three places:

- All DirectAccess client computers need a computer certificate delivered by your enterprise CA. This allows automatic mapping of computer certificates to computer accounts and significantly improves the overall security of the solution. This is the default setting for Forefront UAG DirectAccess, and we highly recommend that you use a Windows Active Directory Certificate Services Certificate Authority and Group Policy to automate deployment of computer certificates through your domain/forest infrastructure.

- The Network location server requires a Web site certificate, because computers configured as DirectAccess clients try to use an SSL connection to the NLS server to determine whether the DirectAccess client is on or off the corporate network. A Windows PKI is not required for generating or deploying the NLS certificate, but it does simplify the task of assigning the certificates to the Web sites. The CRL of the CA that issued this certificate must be available to computers that are configured as DirectAccess clients when those computers are connected to the corporate network.

- The Forefront UAG DirectAccess server needs a Web site certificate to bind to its IP-HTTPS listener. Although you do have the option of using a private PKI, based on your Windows Active Directory Certificate Services CA infrastructure, we highly recommend that you use a commercial certificate to ensure high availability for the CRL listed on the certificate. If the DirectAccess client on the Internet tries to use IP-HTTPS to connect to the Forefront UAG DirectAccess server, and it isn't able to connect to the CRL listed on the certificate, the IP-HTTPS connection will fail.

You can start your private PKI with a single Windows Server 2008 or Windows Server 2008 R2 certificate server. In fact, if your only Windows Server 2008 or above server is the Forefront UAG DirectAccess server, you can use a Windows Server 2003 CA and Windows Server 2003 Active Directory to generate and deploy the certificates. As for the IP-HTTPS certificate, you can use your private PKI for proof of concept and small pilot deployments, but you'll save yourself a lot of trouble if you use a commercial certificate for your production release of DirectAccess.

Network Location Servers

DirectAccess clients use a network location server (NLS) to determine whether they're on or off the corporate network. When you run the Forefront UAG DirectAccess Wizard, it will ask you the name of the NLS. The NLS is a generic SSL Web site that you can install on any Web server; you do not need to use an IIS Web server. The only requirement is that the DirectAccess client on the intranet needs to connect to the NLS Web site and receive a valid HTTP 200 response back. When that HTTP 200 response is received, the DirectAccess client computer will turn off the Name Resolution Policy Table (NRPT) and use the DNS server assigned to its NIC to resolve names on the corporate network. Note that the response must be valid. For more information on this issue, see "What Defines a Functional Connection to a Network Location Server?" at *http://blogs.technet.com/b/tomshinder/archive/2010/07/19 /what-defines-a-functional-connection-to-a-network-location-server.aspx*.

It's important that the NLS is highly available. If the DirectAccess client is on the corporate network, but can't connect to the NLS, then it will believe that it is on the Internet and leave the NRPT enabled. This can be a big problem, because the DirectAccess client will try to use the DirectAccess server's IPv6 address to resolve host names. This might or might not be possible, depending on the configuration of your network. It also depends on whether or not Network Location Awareness (NLA) is able to determine if the DirectAccess client is on the corporate network. If NLA isn't able to determine that the DirectAccess client is on the corporate network, and the NRPT remains enabled, and if there is a path from the corporate network to the external interface of the Forefront UAG DirectAccess server, it's possible that the DirectAccess client located on the corporate network will be able to connect to corporate network resources by looping back into the network through the Forefront UAG DirectAccess server. As you can imagine, if you have a large number of internally located clients doing this, there is the potential for severely bogging down your Internet link.

For this reason, make sure your NLS sites are highly available. You might even want to consider placing extra NLS sites at branch offices, so that, in the event of a site-to-site VPN or WAN link failure, the DirectAccess clients will still be able to connect to the NLS and turn off the NRPT. Of course, if there is a site-to-site VPN or WAN link failure, it might be a good idea to leave the branch office clients DirectAccess enabled, because that might be their only way to reach corporate network resources.

Admin Insight

The entire concept of branch office networks could potentially change with the introduction of DirectAccess. Imagine that all your client systems are configured as DirectAccess clients: branch office clients no longer require a site-to-site VPN or dedicated WAN link to reach the main office. The names of resources situated the branch office can be removed from the NRPT (or just excluded as NRPT exceptions). In that case, the DirectAccess clients will use their locally configured DNS server settings to reach the local resources. If there are no local DNS servers, branch office clients can use NetBIOS (IPv4) or the Local Link Multicast Name Resolution (LLMNR) protocol to reach the local resources. In this scenario, you've removed your dependency on expensive dedicated WAN links and unstable site-to-site VPN links, and replaced them with a general purpose Internet connection. Servers at the branch office can be configured as DirectAccess clients as well, so that they are fully manageable. Even more compelling is the fact that BranchCache is fully supported in a DirectAccess branch office scenario. The potential for simplifying connections and enhancing management and control of the entire IT infrastructure is remarkable!

Certificate Revocation List (CRL) servers

Web servers that host the Certificate Revocation List (CRL) for the certificates used by the NLS and the IP-HTTPS listener need to be made highly available. If the DirectAccess client situated on the corporate network is not able to connect to the CRL location noted on the NLS certificate, the connection attempt will fail, and the DirectAccess client will think that it's on the corporate network and will not turn off its NRPT. If the DirectAccess client on the Internet tries to connect to the IP-HTTPS listener on the external interface of the Forefront UAG DirectAccess server, and it is not able to connect to the CRL location noted on the IP-HTTPS certificate, then the IP-HTTPS connection will fail.

The easiest solution for the IP-HTTPS certificate is to use a commercial CA. The commercial entity will already have a robust infrastructure in place to ensure that the CRL is highly available. You could use a similar strategy with your NLS certificates, but since these are internal servers, you'll be more likely to use your private PKI. In that case, you need to make sure your internal CRL infrastructure is also highly available. You can use any number of methods to make this possible, such as using NLB or an external load balancer. However, it's not a good idea to use a DNS round robin, because if the DNS client is able to resolve the name, it does not traverse the entire list, but rather connects to the first server on the list and does not move to the next entry if the connection attempt fails.

Windows Firewall with Advanced Security and Network Firewalls

Forefront UAG DirectAccess makes liberal use of Windows Firewall with Advanced Security. The Windows Firewall must be enabled on both the Forefront UAG DirectAccess server and DirectAccess clients in order for DirectAccess to work. The reason for this is that the there are firewall rules and connection security rules configured on the Forefront UAG DirectAccess server and on the DirectAccess clients that enable the entire DirectAccess connectivity and authentication model to work.

The connection security rules are used to create the DirectAccess IPsec tunnels between the DirectAccess client and Forefront UAG DirectAccess server. The rules also include the source and destination IP addresses that are allowed and the type of authentication and encryption that is applied to the tunnels. In addition, there are a number of firewall rules that are used to control and direct the type of traffic that is allowed over these tunnels, as well as the traffic that is exempted from IPsec negotiations.

If the Windows Firewall is disabled on either the DirectAccess client or Forefront UAG DirectAccess server, DirectAccess will stop working. This is problematic when administrators, in an attempt to troubleshoot a network problem, turn off the Windows Firewall with Advanced Security on the DirectAccess client or Forefront UAG DirectAccess server. This troubleshooting approach will not work because it completely breaks DirectAccess IPsec tunnel establishment.

The kind of network firewalls you use is up to you and your corporate policy. The Forefront UAG DirectAccess server is designed to be an edge device, which means it can be safely placed on the edge of the corporate network without another firewall in front of it. (I say "another" firewall because the TMG firewall is already on the Forefront UAG server.) However, because the Forefront UAG DirectAccess server is a domain member and many organizations, for one reason or another, require a firewall to be in front of a domain member (regardless of the fact that there is already a firewall on the Forefront UAG DirectAccess server), you will need to consider the way to configure the network firewall in front of the Forefront UAG DirectAccess server.

The network firewall in front of the Forefront UAG DirectAccess server should be configured to:

- Allow IP protocol 41 inbound and outbound to and from the Forefront UAG DirectAccess server's external IP addresses.
- Allow UDP port 3544 inbound and outbound to and from the Forefront UAG DirectAccess server's external IP addresses.
- Allow TCP port 443 inbound and outbound to and from the Forefront UAG DirectAccess server's external IP addresses.

There is no need for back-end servers. The TMG firewall is on the Forefront UAG DirectAccess server and, therefore, acts as both a front-end firewall and a back-end firewall for the Forefront UAG DirectAccess server. However, if policy states that there must be a back-end firewall behind the Forefront UAG DirectAccess server, then you should configure your back-end firewall to allow all IPv4 traffic to and from the internal interface of the Forefront UAG DirectAccess server. In addition, you need to allow IP protocol 41 to and from the internal interface of the Forefront UAG DirectAccess server to support ISATAP communications on your network. Another option is to use IPsec tunnels between the Forefront UAG DirectAccess server and key servers on the internal network, and allow all IP traffic between the Forefront UAG DirectAccess server and all other resources.

 SECURITY ALERT If you fully understand your intranet network application protocol profile, you should consider locking down the protocols you allow through the back-end firewall. Our recommendation is that there is no need for a back-end firewall, and therefore whether you lock down the back-end firewall or not isn't that important. However, for your policies to remain internally consistent, you might want to consider tightening the back-end firewall rules over time, as you understand the traffic profile presented by your DirectAccess clients (which should be similar to the traffic profile presented by your intranet clients, because they will have the same level of access). Another alternative is to use IPsec policies to control traffic to back-end resources.

Remote Access VPN Servers

DirectAccess will be able to meet almost all the needs your remote users have. However, as we have pointed out in other sections of this chapter, there can be certain limitations introduced into the Forefront UAG DirectAccess solution by the deployment details. For example, we've seen that there are certain limitations to an IPv4-only network. In addition, some client applications are not IPv6-capable, so even though NAT64/DNS64 could solve the connectivity issue to an IPv4-only server, you would continue to have the problem that the client side of the client/server application needs to be IPv6-aware.

For those circumstances in which the Forefront UAG DirectAccess solution will not work for specific applications, you will need to provide alternate methods in order to allow your users to access those applications. The solution will depend on the nature of the particular client/server application. For example, at the time we are writing this book, the OCS client will not work with the NAT64/DNS64 solution, because the protocol it uses embeds an IPv4 address that the NAT64/DNS64 protocol translator can't interpret. Therefore, you need to provide an alternate method for accessing the OCS server from the Communicator client. One way you can do this is to use an Internet-accessible OCS proxy and configure the NRPT so that that proxy is not reachable through the Forefront UAG DirectAccess tunnels.

However, not all applications make it possible to set up Internet-accessible proxies. In these cases, you will want to consider making VPN access available to users. Remote access VPN client connectivity is also useful for non-DirectAccess-capable clients, such as Windows XP and Windows Vista. If you already have a VPN solution in place, you can certainly use it. However, if you want to consolidate your remote access solutions, you might consider co-locating your remote access VPN client connectivity solution with the Forefront UAG DirectAccess solution.

This is actually consistent with the preferred method for deploying Forefront UAG DirectAccess arrays. Forefront UAG provides three key enabling scenarios:

- Reverse Web proxy and Web portal access
- DirectAccess
- Remote access client VPN

If you choose to use all of the functionality included with Forefront UAG, you should consider separating the reverse Web proxy and Web portal access array from the DirectAccess and remote access VPN client array. You can co-locate the Forefront UAG DirectAccess server and the Forefront UAG SSTP server on the same machine. The SSTP server will support clients using Windows Vista SP1 and above. However, SSTP is not supported by Windows XP, so if you want to provide remote access for the Windows XP clients, you might consider requiring them to use the reverse Web proxy or portal applications. Given the higher threat that Windows XP presents to networks today, even when those networks are comprehensively managed, enforcing a least-privilege stance on the Windows XP clients by forcing them to use the Web proxy or portal experience might be the best decision overall.

 SECURITY ALERT **Forefront UAG leverages RRAS and TMG to make SSTP connections available, but that does not give you the granular access control over the SSTP connections that you have when you deploy the TMG SSTP VPN solution. If you require this level of granular control, you might want to consider deploying a separate array of TMG firewalls that can be used for outbound access control and SSTP remote access VPN client accessibility.**

DirectAccess Security Considerations

At this point, you might be thinking that DirectAccess is just what you need to make your systems more manageable and your users more productive. However, since this is a relatively new technology, you might also be wondering about the security issues it introduces. After all, the DirectAccess client is connected to the corporate network when the DirectAccess client machine is turned on, even before the user logs on. What are the security implications of this kind of always-on state?

One way to look at the relative security issues involved with the DirectAccess client is to consider the ways in which the DirectAccess client's threat profile might differ from the profiles of other clients that you manage. Let's assume that there are three general types of clients that are domain members under your administrative control. These are:

- The bolted-in corporate network client
- The roaming remote access VPN client
- The DirectAccess client

The Bolted-in Corporate Network Client

The bolted-in corporate network client is a system that never leaves the confines of the corporate network. This system is a domain member, is always managed, and is never exposed to any other networks. Its Internet access is always controlled by an application layer inspection firewall, such as a TMG firewall; USB and other removable media slots are either administratively or physically locked down; and physical access to the building is allowed only to employees and escorted guests. These systems also have anti-malware software installed; are configured through Group Policy or some other management system to maintain desired security configuration; and have Network Access Protection (NAP) or a similar network access control (NAC) solution enabled, in order to prevent rogue systems from connecting to the network and accessing corporate resources. Windows Firewall with Advanced Security is enabled and configured to reduce the risk introduced by network worms.

This concept of the bolted-in client gets as close to the ideal of a secure client as one can imagine:

- The system is never exposed to untrusted networks.
- The system is always managed.
- The system is always under the control of corporate IT.
- Access to the system is limited to employees and escorted guests.
- Out of band access to the system is limited because ports for removable media are administratively or physically disabled.
- An application layer inspection Internet firewall, such as TMG, prevents users from downloading exploits from over the Internet.
- NAP or another NAC solution reduces the risks of unmanaged clients connecting to the network and spreading malware obtained from other networks.

While you might imagine this to be the ideal system in terms of network security, how realistic is this characterization? How many systems (other than servers) do you have now that never leave the corporate network? Finally, even with these controls in place, is this machine immune from attack?

- Social engineering is a common method attackers use to gain physical access to specifically targeted machines so that malware and Trojans can be installed on bolted-in clients.

- Even with physical ports disabled, it's likely that users will be given access to at least an optical drive, in which case malware obtained from an outside venue can find its way onto the bolted-in client.

- An application layer inspection firewall can go a long way to preventing malware and Trojans from entering the corporate network. However, if the firewall doesn't perform outbound SSL (HTTPS) inspection, it is essentially worthless, because Trojans can use the secure (and uninspected) SSL channel to reach their controllers.

- If a Trojan were installed on the bolted-in client, a well-written Trojan would use HTTP or SSL to connect to its controller and would most likely connect to a site that has not yet been categorized by URL filtering solutions and thus would not be blocked. Even if the organization used an "Allow List" approach to security, the attacker could hijack a low profile "safe site" (perhaps with DNS poisoning) and instruct the Trojan to connect to that site so that it can receive control commands.

- If users are using wireless connections, they can easily disconnect from the corporate wireless and connect to a tethered phone to access resources that are blocked by the corporate firewall. They can then reconnect to the corporate network when they get what they want. Users with either a wireless or wired connection could easily plug in a wireless air card to connect to an unfiltered network and compromise the machine through the alternate gateway.

It's important to understand that this information is not presented to suggest that performing security due-diligence is a lesson in futility. Instead, what should be clear is that even in the ideal situation in which the corporate network client is bolted in, there are a lot of things that can go wrong and can lead to security incidents. You still need to do everything you can to make sure that your machines are secure, up to date, and well-managed, but you should also put into perspective the way these isolated and immobile corporate network clients compare with other types of corporate client systems.

Finally, it's worth considering whether or not the concept of the bolted-in client might be of academic interest only. How many of these clients exist on corporate networks today, especially networks on which the majority of employees are knowledge workers? In a task worker environment, you might think of Virtual Desktop Infrastructure (VDI) as a viable solution, because the tasks the employees perform don't require the wide array of functionality provided by a full PC environment, but knowledge workers need the flexibility and power provided by fully enabled PC platforms to give them the ability to provide their companies advantages over the competition.

The Roaming Remote Access VPN Client

In the 1990s, the bolted-in client was the norm. Today, the bolted-in client has given way to the roaming remote access VPN client. Knowledge workers have powerful laptop computers they take to work, to their homes, to customer sites, to hotels, to conferences, to airports, and to anywhere else in the world where there is an Internet connection. Additionally, in many cases, after being to one or more of these locations, they bring their laptops back to the corporate network.

The roaming remote access VPN client poses a very different threat profile when compared to the mythical bolted-in client. These machines are domain members, have anti-malware software installed, have the Windows Firewall with Advanced Security enabled, and are initially configured to be fully compliant with corporate security policy. The roaming VPN client computer, when first delivered to the user, is as secure as any other computer on the corporate network.

But that state doesn't last for long. The user might not connect to the corporate network over the VPN connection for days or weeks. Or the user might connect daily for a week or two, and then not connect for a few months. In the interim, the roaming VPN client computer slowly but surely falls out of compliance. Group policy is not updated, antivirus updates might not be installed on a regular basis, other anti-malware software may fall out of date, and security and compliance controls that are exercised on clients located on the corporate network never find their way to the roaming remote access VPN clients, because the users fail to connect over the VPN in a timely manner.

As the roaming VPN client falls further and further out of your defined security compliance configuration, the problem becomes magnified, because the machine is connected to a number of networks of low and unknown trust. These unmanaged or poorly managed networks might be filled with network worms, or with users who have physical or logical access to the computer but who would not have access to the computer if it were to never leave the corporate network.

Worst of all, when the user brings the computer back to the corporate network it is unleashed on the rest of the network. The damage might be limited if you have NAP or a similar NAC solution enabled on the network, but how many networks have actually deployed these technologies?

As you can see, the roaming VPN client suffers from a number of security issues compared to the bolted in client:

- The roaming VPN client is connected to the corporate network on an intermittent basis, or sometimes never, and therefore falls out of the reach of Group Policy and other management systems.

- The roaming VPN client is exposed to unmanaged and poorly managed networks, increasing the potential attack surface to which the roaming remote access VPN client is exposed.

- The roaming VPN client can access the Internet, and the user can do whatever the user wants while connected to Internet sites, because there is typically no filtering of Internet connections when the VPN client is not connected to the corporate network.

- If the VPN client is configured to disable split tunneling, it might be forced to use corporate Internet access gateways during the time the client is connected. However, once the VPN connection is dropped, the user can do what the user wants to do, again, and can share any malware or Trojans obtained when disconnected from the VPN when the connection is established again.

■ Users sometimes avoid connecting to the VPN because logon times are slow, connectivity is inconsistent, and the entire VPN experience is less than optimal, further increasing the risk of falling out of security compliance and increasing the risk of compromise.

The roaming VPN client is, therefore, significantly different from the bolted-in client from a security perspective because:

■ Group policy might or might not be updated on a timely basis.

■ Antivirus software might or might not be updated on a timely basis.

■ Anti-malware software might or might not be updated on a timely basis.

■ Other management and control methods might or might not be able to reconfigure the client on a timely basis.

■ The number of people who have access to the physical machine is potentially greater than the number of people who have access to a bolted-in client's machine. Access is also extended to people who might even steal the machine.

The key differences between the roaming VPN client and the bolted-in client are that the VPN client is not always managed and that it is exposed to a greater number of programmatic and physical threats. Many companies have already introduced methods to mitigate these threats:

■ Disk encryption, such as BitLocker, is deployed so that if a machine is stolen, the disk can't be read using an offline attack.

■ Disk encryption can also employ key-based disk access controls, so that if the machine is turned off, the machine will not boot without the key.

■ Two-factor authentication is required to log on to a machine, and the second factor is also required to unlock the machine or wake it from sleep.

■ NAP or similar technologies are deployed to test endpoint security before the machine is allowed corporate network access. If the machine cannot remediate, it is not allowed corporate network access.

■ User accounts used to log into the network are not the same as administrative accounts used to manage network servers and services; this prevents elevation attacks.

■ The datacenter is pushed back from both VPN and intranet clients, so that the datacenter is physically and logically separated from the entire client population.

Using one of more of these mitigations will go a long way to reducing the potential threats exposed by remote access VPN clients. While perhaps not raising the VPN client's security to the level of the bolted-in client's security, there might be scenarios in which the roaming remote access VPN client can actually present a lower risk. We will examine one of those scenarios later in this chapter.

The DirectAccess Client

Now we come to the subject of the DirectAccess client. As in the case of the VPN client, this computer can move from the corporate network to a hotel room, to a conference center, to an airport, and to anywhere else that a roaming remote access VPN client might be located. The DirectAccess client, in its lifetime, will be connected to both trusted and untrusted networks, just as the roaming remote access VPN client will, and the risk of physical compromise of the computer is also similar. Thus, it would appear that the DirectAccess client and the VPN client are essentially the same from a threat perspective.

However, there are some significant differences between the roaming remote access VPN client and the DirectAccess client:

- The DirectAccess client is always managed. As long as the DirectAccess client computer is on, it will have connectivity with management servers that keep it within the organization's security configuration compliance.

- The DirectAccess client is always serviceable. If IT needs to connect to the DirectAccess client to perform custom software configuration or troubleshoot an issue, there is no problem getting access, because the connection between the DirectAccess client and IT management stations is bidirectional.

- The DirectAccess client has access only to the management and configuration infrastructure through the first tunnel. General network access isn't available until the user logs on and creates the infrastructure tunnel.

When you compare the DirectAccess client to the remote access VPN client it appears that the DirectAccess client presents a much lower threat profile than the VPN client, because the DirectAccess client is always within the command and control of corporate IT. This is in contrast to the roaming remote access VPN clients that might or might not connect to the corporate network for long periods of time, leading to configuration entropy that can significantly increase the risk of system compromise. In addition, the mitigations that apply to the remote access VPN client, described in the previous section, can also be used with the DirectAccess client.

Here we reach the point of making a critical distinction: when comparing the roaming remote access VPN client to the DirectAccess client, all the evidence indicates that the DirectAccess client poses a lower threat profile. Comparisons between the DirectAccess client and the bolted-in client are of academic interest only, because few organizations have bolted-in clients anymore, and most firms are giving users VPN access to reach corporate network resources. Also, both VPN clients and DirectAccess clients will move in and out of the corporate network, making the division between the corporate network client and the remote client virtually meaningless from a security perspective.

The First Tunnel Issue

Some administrators are concerned about the first (infrastructure) tunnel always being active, because if the first tunnel is always active it can be used to leverage attacks against the network. That concern is amplified by the fact that mobile computers are often lost or stolen, so that an intruder can take advantage of this situation to gain access to corporate resources. Some important considerations regarding the first tunnel include:

- The infrastructure tunnel is established using the context of the machine account.
- The infrastructure tunnel cannot be leveraged to start the intranet tunnel to increase the scope of access.
- BitLocker can be used to prevent an intruder from gaining disk access during system startup; this includes waking the system from hibernation.
- Network Access Protection can be used to prevent the second tunnel from being established when the NAP process determines that the client system is not healthy.
- Smart cards can be required to wake the system from sleep or to unlock the computer.
- The infrastructure tunnel represents a much lower security risk than a remote access VPN connection. The remote access VPN connection works within the context of a logged-on user account and has access to all systems on the corporate network, in contrast to the DirectAccess infrastructure tunnel connection, which works within the context of the machine account and only has access to selected infrastructure and management servers on the network.

The concern about the first tunnel being always on doesn't take into account the fact that modern malware has kept pace with advances in software development across all sectors. Like many legitimate applications, malware can be, and is, written to be tolerant of systems that are in a disconnected state. Then, when the malware detects that the system is connected, it can launch the attack. This is true of roaming remote access VPN clients. Given that these kinds of asynchronous and automated attacks are relatively easy for malware writers to instantiate, there is no practical difference between the always-on DirectAccess client and the remote access VPN client. The important point here is that the DirectAccess client poses no more risk than a remote access VPN client, and because the DirectAccess client is comprehensively managed, it ends up being less likely to be compromised.

What about Split Tunneling?

By default, the Forefront UAG DirectAccess client uses split tunneling to allow access to the corporate network over the IPsec DirectAccess tunnels and a direct connection to the Internet for non-corporate network-based requests. This is accomplished by leveraging the Name Resolution Policy Table. Recall that the NRTP contains strings for host names or FQDNs, and when there is a match, the name query request is sent to the IP address of the DNS server listed on the NRPT. That server is going to be the Forefront UAG DirectAccess server, which performs a DNS proxy action for the DirectAccess client.

Some DirectAccess administrators might be concerned about the prospect of split tunneling because in the early 1990s they likely encountered issues with remote access VPN clients routing or bridging connections between an attacker on the Internet and resources on the corporate network. While this routing has been disabled on modern Windows clients, the concern about split tunneling remains.

What if an intruder was able to somehow take control of a DirectAccess computer by being able to bridge a connection between a computer on the Internet and the DirectAccess client? The result would be failure; the remote attacker would not be able to establish a DirectAccess tunnel because the IPsec tunnel between the attacker's computer and the DirectAccess server would not be established.

However, some administrators believe there are other methods that attackers can use to benefit from split tunneling. For example, suppose split tunneling is enabled on a remote access VPN client and an attacker is able to use social engineering to get the user to download and install a Trojan? That Trojan is configured to call the intruder's Trojan controller computer to download instructions or allow the attacker access so that real time commands can be issued. In this way, the attacker will be able to attack resources on the corporate network when split tunneling is enabled and the user's computer is connected to both the attacker (via the Trojan) and the corporate network. In this scenario, the attacker doesn't need to have the DirectAccess client establish the connection to reach the corporate network.

But what if split tunneling were disabled? Would this change the scenario? For example, suppose the Trojan initiates a connection with its control server when the remote access VPN client is not connected to the corporate network over the VPN, and then the user starts up a VPN connection. Just starting the VPN connection will not automatically disconnect the established session between the Trojan and the attacker. Therefore, in this scenario, disabling split tunneling has conferred no security advantage.

Let's look at another example. Suppose the attacker has taken control of the DirectAccess client computer. The attacker could then enable split tunneling on the client side, or, if that is not possible, it is relatively simple to create static routes that will enable the Trojan to connect to the control server even when the VPN connection is up and split tunneling is disabled.

This brings up the issue of a completely "rooted" system. In this case, the system is under the complete control of the attacker. The attacker has the ability to elevate privileges and perform any chosen operation on the compromised computer. In this worst-case scenario, what is the difference between the DirectAccess client, the roaming remote access VPN client, and the bolted-in client? Indeed, in this worst-case scenario, one could argue that the bolted-in client (assuming that such clients exist) poses the greatest threat, because the comprehensive security measures deployed on DirectAccess and VPN clients might not be implemented on a bolted-in client. They might not be implemented because of a mistaken belief that corporate network clients are inherently more trustworthy and clients that are not on the corporate network cannot be trusted.

The goal of this discussion is not to say that a DirectAccess client cannot be compromised. Instead, the points we are trying to make are that the DirectAccess client represents a threat profile similar to, or lower than, a compromised roaming remote access VPN client and perhaps even less than the bolted-in client (especially in a worst-case scenario), and that split tunneling, whether enabled or disabled, ends up making relatively little difference in terms of the likelihood of such compromise.

Summary of the DirectAccess Client Security Model

The Forefront UAG DirectAccess solution is relatively new, so it's expected that there will be questions about the security issues that it brings to the fore. While, in many respects, DirectAccess presents itself as being similar to a roaming remote access VPN client solution, its security posture is different enough to qualify it as a unique solution.

There are several conclusions we can make about DirectAccess security and the DirectAccess security model:

- The infrastructure tunnel requires mutual computer certificate authentication and computer account authentication using NTLMv2.
- The infrastructure tunnel provides access only to infrastructure and management servers that are specified when the Forefront UAG DirectAccess Wizard is run.
- Any communications moving over the infrastructure tunnel are done within the context of the computer account.
- NAP can be used as an endpoint detection method to confirm that the DirectAccess client meets corporate security requirements before the intranet tunnel is established.
- The intranet tunnel requires mutual computer certificate authentication and user authentication using Kerberos.
- Access to the intranet tunnel can be limited by requiring two-factor authentication, such as requiring that the user have a smart card to log on or to bring the computer out of locked state.
- BitLocker can be deployed to help mitigate the threat of a physical attack against the DirectAccess client. If the intruder restarts the computer, a Personal Identification Number (PIN) can be required to gain access to the hard disk; similarly, if the computer is configured to hibernate, a PIN can be required to bring the machine out of hibernation.
- The threat profile presented by the DirectAccess computer is lower than that presented by a roaming remote access VPN client, because the DirectAccess client is always managed.
- The threat profile presented by the DirectAccess computer, in a worst case scenario, might be superior to that presented by a bolted-in client (assuming that such a client computer exists on enterprise networks today), because greater measures have been extended to secure the DirectAccess computer. Some administrators mistakenly believe that corporate network clients are inherently more trustworthy than remote or roaming clients.
- The always-on nature of the DirectAccess infrastructure tunnel has been interpreted to be more of a security issue than it really is, because security specialists know that modern malware developers keep up with industry coding practices and create malware that is resilient in disconnected scenarios and is able to easily launch attacks when

network connectivity is established (in a VPN scenario or returning to the corporate network scenario).

- Although split tunneling was an issue in the early days of VPN networking, it no longer presents a significant threat, because malware developers are able to easily circumvent scenarios in which split tunneling is disabled in both real-time and asynchronous and automated attacks against corporate network resources.

Forefront UAG 2010 DirectAccess Requirements

The Forefront UAG DirectAccess solution is very flexible, so there are not a lot of requirements for creating a fully working Forefront UAG solution. The minimal requirements for a working DirectAccess solution are:

- At least one Forefront UAG DirectAccess server running on Windows Server 2008 R2 (more Windows Server 2008 R2 servers are required if you wish to create a Forefront UAG DirectAccess array).
- At least two consecutive public IP addresses bound to the external interface of the Forefront UAG DirectAccess server or array. If you create an array, you will need at least two consecutive IP addresses that will be shared among all members of the array and one dedicated IP address that is assigned to each member of the array. The total number of public IP addresses required for the external interface of the array is equal to the number of servers in the array plus two.
- DirectAccess clients must run Windows 7 Enterprise or Ultimate Edition.
- At least one domain controller running Windows Server 2003 or above.
- A DNS server of any type. If you want to benefit from the full manage-out scenario and bidirectional communications between the DirectAccess client and management services on the corporate network, then you should have a DNS server that is able to accept dynamic registrations of IPv6 addresses from the DirectAccess clients and servers on your corporate network (the IPv6 addresses on the corporate network can be ISATAP addresses).
- An internal Public Key Infrastructure that can deploy computer certificates to domain member DirectAccess clients. DirectAccess clients must be domain members. You can use Group Policy autoenrollment to deploy the computer certificates.
- An internal or external PKI to assign Web site certificates to network location servers. In general, you will want to use an internal PKI for this, but this is not a requirement. The CRL for the NLS certificates must be available to all internal network clients.
- An internal or external PKI to support the IP-HTTPS certificate. In general, you will want to use a public certificate provider because they have already implemented a highly available CRL deployment.

Notice that Windows Server 2008 R2 is required only for the DirectAccess server array. There is no other requirement for Windows Server 2008 R2. That means that your network can be running Windows 2000, Windows XP, Windows Server 2003, Windows Server 2008, or Windows Server 2008 R2, and you can have a working Forefront UAG DirectAccess deployment. However, keep in mind that servers that are not IPv6-capable will not be able to manage-out your DirectAccess clients.

Forefront UAG 2010 DirectAccess Configuration Wizard

The Forefront UAG DirectAccess Wizard configures many of the components of the DirectAccess solution for you. When you run the Forefront UAG DirectAccess Wizard, the following takes place:

- The Forefront UAG DirectAccess server is configured as an ISATAP router.
- The Forefront UAG DirectAccess server is configured as a Teredo server and relay.
- The Forefront UAG DirectAccess server is configured as a 6to4 router.
- The Forefront UAG DirectAccess server is configured as an IP-HTTPS server.
- The Forefront UAG DirectAccess Wizard creates Group Policy Objects (GPOs) that contain DirectAccess client settings and DirectAccess server settings that control the Windows Firewall with Advanced Security Connection security and firewall rules.
- The Forefront UAG DirectAccess Wizard deploys the GPOs to the DirectAccess servers' and DirectAccess clients' security groups.

The following section provides a detailed discussion of the Forefront UAG DirectAccess Wizard. However, before you can get a fully working DirectAccess solution, there are a number of key infrastructure elements and configuration requirements that need to be deployed and completed. For a detailed account of the way to set up a Forefront UAG DirectAccess solution in a test lab, see "Test Lab Guide: Demonstrate Forefront UAG DirectAccess Network Load Balancing and Array Configuration," at *http://www.microsoft.com/downloads/details .aspx?displaylang=en&FamilyID=7fb64cad-5dac-471a-9fbf-a6c9d03ffbad*. The following discussion of the Forefront UAG DirectAccess is based on the configuration used in the Test Lab Guide.

Running the Forefront UAG DirectAccess Wizard

The Forefront UAG DirectAccess Wizard makes it easier to install and configure many of the components of the DirectAccess solution. The wizard will create Group Policy Objects that configure the Forefront UAG DirectAccess server and the DirectAccess clients to enable the required IPv6 networking technologies and Windows Firewall with Advanced Security connection security rules that are required for IPsec connectivity. In this section, we'll take a look at the Forefront UAG DirectAccess Wizard. For detailed instructions on ways to create a working Forefront UAG test lab, see the Test Lab Guide mentioned earlier.

> **NOTE** The following is a walkthrough of the Forefront UAG DirectAccess Wizard only. Performing the steps in this section will not create a working Forefront UAG DirectAccess deployment. For detailed information on creating a working Forefront UAG DirectAccess deployment in a test lab, see "Test Lab Guide: Demonstrate Forefront UAG DirectAccess," at *http://www.microsoft.com/downloads/en/details.aspx?displaylang=en&FamilyID =c243c30c-6476-4061-9520-124710dbdd27* and "Test Lab Guide: Demonstrate Forefront UAG DirectAccess Network Load Balancing and Array Configuration," at *http://www.microsoft.com/downloads/details.aspx?displaylang=en&FamilyID=7fb64cad -5dac-471a-9fbf-a6c9d03ffbad.*

The Forefront UAG DirectAccess Wizard is available in the Forefront UAG Management console. In the left pane of the Forefront UAG console, click the DirectAccess node. In the right pane of the console, you'll see the Forefront UAG DirectAccess Configuration pane, as shown in Figure 5-1.

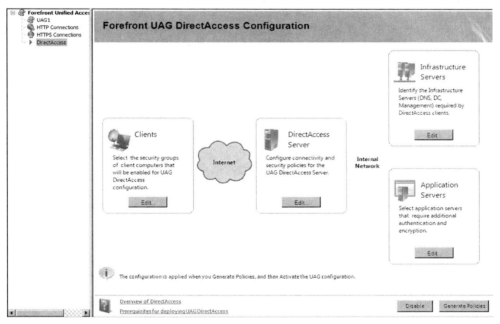

FIGURE 5-1

In the Clients section, click Edit (the name on the button will be "Configure" if you have not configured DirectAccess yet, and it will be "Edit" if you have already configured DirectAccess on the server; in this example, we have already configured the array, so it says "Edit"), as shown in Figure 5-2.

FIGURE 5-2

On the Forefront UAG DirectAccess Client Configuration page, enter the name of the group or groups of computers to which your DirectAccess client computer accounts belong. You will have to create these groups yourself; the DirectAccess Wizard does not do this for you. Click Add, and the Select Group dialog box will appear. This is where you enter the names of the group or groups that contain the machines that you want to be DirectAccess clients, as shown in Figure 5-3. The DirectAccess GPOs will be applied to these groups using Group Policy security filtering.

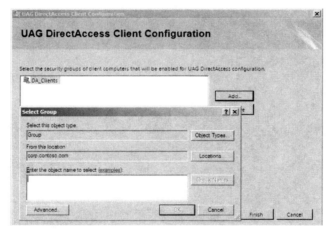

FIGURE 5-3

The next step is to configure the DirectAccess server settings. In the DirectAccess Server box, click Configure or Edit to configure connectivity and security policies for the Forefront UAG DirectAccess server, as shown in Figure 5-4.

DirectAccess
Server

Configure connectivity and
security policies for the
UAG DirectAccess Server.

Edit...

FIGURE 5-4

If you have already configured a Forefront UAG DirectAccess array, the first step on the
Forefront UAG DirectAccess Server Configuration Wizard will be to assess whether or not your
array can support NLB. (If you have not yet configured the array, the first screen you will see is
the one shown in Figure 5-6.) Notice that there are two options on this page:

- **Windows Network Load Balancing**   When you select this option, high-availability
  will be enabled using the integrated NLB feature included with Windows, which has
  been customized to work with DirectAccess. Note that while Forefront UAG supports unicast, multicast, and IGMP multicast NLB, if you want to enable NLB for the
  DirectAccess array, you will have to use unicast. If you want to deploy Forefront UAG
  DirectAccess in a virtual environment, Hyper-V supports unicast NLB.

- **External Load Balancing**   Use this option if you want to use an external load balancer. In this case the NLB features will not be enabled.

If everything is in place, a validation box will appear, saying The Array Has All The Required
Prerequisites For The Selected Load Balancing Method, as shown in Figure 5-5.

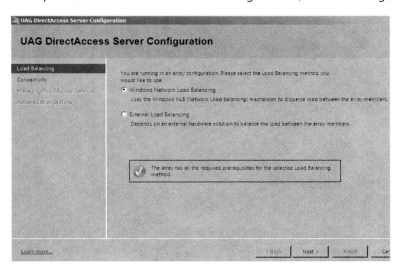

FIGURE 5-5

On the Connectivity page of the Forefront UAG DirectAccess Server Configuration page, configure the IP addresses used on the internal and external interfaces of the Forefront UAG server. On the Internet-facing section, select the first of the two consecutive IP addresses on the external interface of the Forefront UAG server. Two consecutive public IP addresses are required for Teredo to work, and if you don't configure the Forefront UAG server or array to use two consecutive public IP addresses, the wizard will call out an error condition. Notice that after you select the first address, the second address appears.

In the Internal section, select the IP address on the internal interface of the Forefront UAG DirectAccess server. In almost all cases, you'll have single IP address on the internal interface. If you are using native IPv6 addressing, you'll have the option to select an Internal IPv6 Address. If not, the Forefront UAG DirectAccess server will be configured as an ISATAP router, and it will assign itself an IPv6 ISATAP address.

As shown in Figure 5-6, there is an important note at the bottom of the page:

ISATAP IPv6 transition technologies will be enabled on the Forefront UAG DirectAccess server. Register the DNS name "ISATAP" with [addresses] on the DNS in all domains to enable IPv6 connectivity on these domains. In addition, ensure that ISATAP is not blocked in the Global Query Block List on all DNS servers.

This is an important notice, because the ISATAP hosts on the internal network need to be able to resolve the name ISATAP to an IP address on the internal interface of the Forefront UAG DirectAccess server in order to obtain information about the way to configure their own ISATAP adapters. To do this, the ISATAP hosts on the internal network need to resolve the name ISATAP. By default, Windows DNS servers will drop queries to the name ISATAP, so you need to use the dnscmd command to enable queries for ISATAP. You can find more information on how to do this in "Managing the Global Query Block List," at *http://technet.microsoft .com/en-us/library/cc794902(WS.10).aspx.*

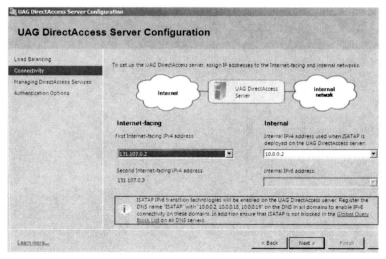

FIGURE 5-6

On the next page of the wizard, you are given the option to enable DNS64 and NAT64. These two technologies allow you to have IPv4-only hosts on the internal network, as shown in Figure 5-7. If you don't have these IPv6-to-IPv4 protocol translator technologies enabled, the DirectAccess client on the Internet won't be able to communicate with IPv4-only servers or services. The reason is that the DirectAccess client always uses IPv6 to communicate with resources through the Forefront UAG DirectAccess server. However, the Forefront UAG DirectAccess server that has DNS64 and NAT64 enabled will be able to spoof the addresses of the IPv4-only servers and allow the DirectAccess clients to communicate with those servers.

In most cases, you'll want to leave these technologies enabled. However, if you have a native IPv6 infrastructure on your corporate network, you won't need these, so you can turn them off and reduce your overhead.

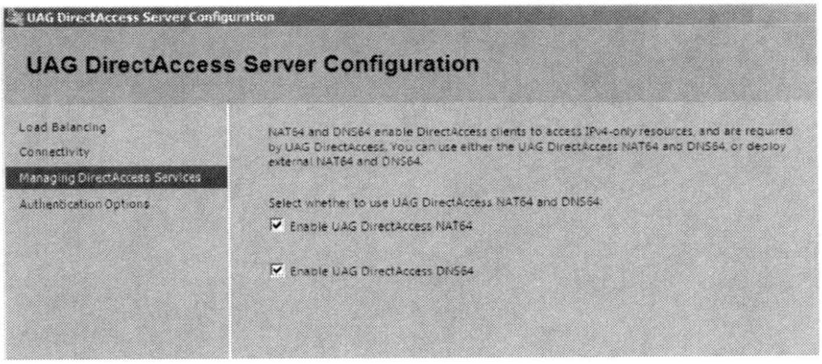

FIGURE 5-7

On the Authentication Options page of the Forefront UAG DirectAccess Server Configuration page, select the certificate that will be used as the root certificate that verifies certificates sent by DirectAccess clients and is used as the root certificate for the IP-HTTPS listener.

In the Browse And Select A Root Or Intermediate Certificate That Verifies Certificates Sent By DirectAccess Clients section, you can select either Use Root Certificate or Use Intermediate Certificate. After making that selection, click Browse and select the certificate, as shown in Figures 5-8 and 5-9.

In the Select The Certificate That Authenticates The Forefront UAG DirectAccess Server To A Client Connecting Using IP-HTTPS section, which will be similar to the page shown in Figure 5-8, click Browse to select the certificate that will be used by the IP-HTTPS listener, as shown in Figure 5-9. The DirectAccess Wizard does not create this certificate; you will need to create this certificate before running the DirectAccess Wizard.

There are two more options available on this page:

- **Clients That Log On Using A PKI Smart Card** This option, when selected, will force users to use a smart card that contains the user's certificate. Microsoft uses this option for their own DirectAccess deployment.

- **Computers That Comply With Your Organization's NAP Policy**   If you have NAP deployed on your network, the DirectAccess client computer will only be allowed network access if it passes the security checks performed by your NAP policies.

Note that your smart card and NAP infrastructures need to be in place before they will work with DirectAccess. The DirectAccess Wizard does not configure these services, but if they are in place, the Forefront UAG DirectAccess server will work with them when you select these options.

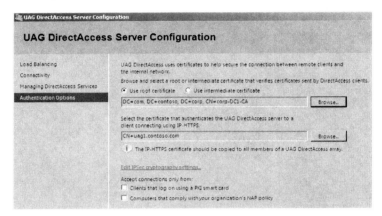

FIGURE 5-8

FIGURE 5-9

The next step is to configure the Infrastructure Servers. Click Edit in the Infrastructure Servers box, as shown in Figure 5-10, to identify the infrastructure servers, such as DNS, domain controllers, and management servers, that will be required by DirectAccess clients.

FIGURE 5-10

In the Infrastructure Server Configuration Wizard, on the Network Location Server page, enter the FQDN of the Network Location Server or NLS. The DirectAccess client uses the NLS to determine whether it's on the corporate network or off the corporate network. If the DirectAccess client can connect to the NLS using an SSL connection, the DirectAccess client assumes that it is on the corporate network and turns off its DirectAccess client components. If the DirectAccess client cannot connect to the NLS server using an SSL connection, it assumes that it is off the intranet, and will turn on its DirectAccess client components and connect to the network through the Forefront UAG DirectAccess sever.

In Figure 5-11 you can see that the DirectAccess client has been configured with an NLS server. You can click Validate to confirm that the client can connect to the NLS server. As it says on this page, "It is recommended that you use a highly available network location sever. If the HTTPS URL is unavailable, client connectivity may be disrupted." This is an important point, and you must make sure that your NLS servers are highly available; if they are not, depending on your deployment, DirectAccess clients that are moved to the corporate network will not be able to connect to key resources, such as domain controllers.

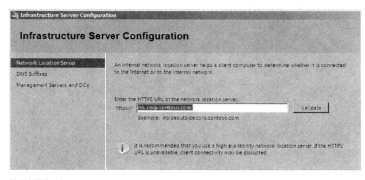

FIGURE 5-11

On the DNS Suffixes page, you configure the DNS suffixes for names that should be sent over the DirectAccess tunnel. The DirectAccess Wizard will automatically configure key entries for you, but you can add more if you like. This is the configuration interface for the NRPT, which the DirectAccess client uses to determine the names that should be resolved as names for resources on the corporate network, and the names that should be resolved as resources available on the Internet.

> **NOTE** For a detailed account of the way the DirectAccess client uses the NRPT, see Tom's blog post, "DirectAccess Client Location Awareness — NRPT Name Resolution," The Edge Man blog, at *http://blogs.technet.com/tomshinder/archive/2010/04/02/directaccess-client-location-awareness-nrpt-name-resolution.aspx*.

As shown in Figure 5-12, there are also three options at the bottom of these pages that let you determine the way name resolution should be handled when a name query fails. These are:

- Only Use Local Name Resolution If The Name Does Not Exist In DNS (Most Restrictive)
- Fall Back To Local Name Resolution If The Name Does Not Exist In DNS Or The DNS Servers Are Unreachable When The Client Computer Is On A Private Network (Recommended)
- Fall Back To Local Name Resolution For Any Kind Of DNS Resolution Error (Least Secure)

Note here that Local Name Resolution refers to resolution of single-label names. If the query failure is for a FQDN, there is no fail back for name resolution.

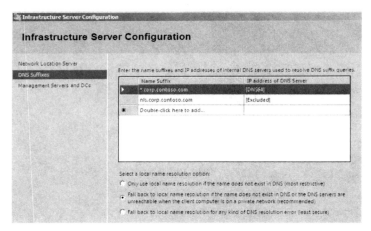

FIGURE 5-12

On the Management Servers And DCs page, configure the management servers and domain controllers that need to be reachable by the DirectAccess client when the DirectAccess client is connecting over the infrastructure DirectAccess IPsec tunnel. Notice that the Forefront UAG DirectAccess Wizard will automatically detect the domain controllers, as seen in Figure 5-13. If you want to add more domains or more servers (such as SCCM or other management servers), click Add Server or Add Domain.

One important issue to consider is that the machines listed on this page are accessible over the infrastructure tunnel. The DirectAccess client establishes the infrastructure tunnel before the user logs onto the computer, using a computer certificate and NTLMv2 authentication with the computer's account in Active Directory. The infrastructure tunnel is a bidirectional tunnel so that the DirectAccess client is reachable from the corporate network. Therefore, if IT needs to connect to the DirectAccess client for management or control, they can do that over the infrastructure tunnel, even when the user is not logged on. There are some other requirements to get this manage-out connectivity to work the way you want it to. For more information on configuring Forefront UAG DirectAccess to support manage out scenarios, see "Test Lab Guide: Demonstrate Forefront UAG DirectAccess Remote Management," at *http://www.microsoft.com/downloads/details.aspx?displaylang=en&FamilyID =385a3144-8e84-4335-896b-a2927e4d46cd.*

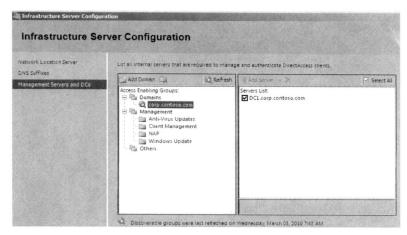

FIGURE 5-13

The last step is to configure the Application Servers. Click Edit in the Application Servers box, as shown in Figure 5-14, to select application servers that might require additional authentication or encryption.

FIGURE 5-14

On the Application Server Configuration page, there are two options, as shown in Figure 5-15:

- **Require End-To-Edge Authentication And Encryption**   This option establishes a secure IPsec tunnel between the DirectAccess client and the Forefront UAG DirectAccess server. After terminating the connection at the Forefront UAG DirectAccess sever, the communications are passed "in the clear" on the corporate network.

- **Require End-To-End Authentication And Encryption To Specified Application Servers**   This option allows you to take advantage of IPsec transport mode connections between the DirectAccess client and destination servers on the corporate network. If there are servers on the corporate network that require a secure connection from end-to-end, then select this option and select the server for which the end-to-end secure connection is required.

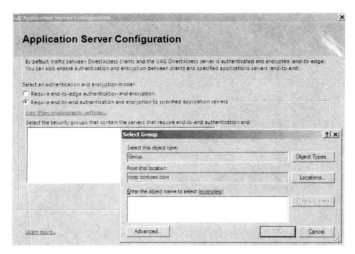

FIGURE 5-15

When you click the Edit IPsec Cryptography Settings link, you can see the default IPsec settings for the end-to-end tunnel between the DirectAccess client and the secure servers on the corporate network, as shown in Figure 5-16. Notice that ESP is the default protocol, SHA-256 is used at the integrity algorithm (hash protocol), and NULL encryption is used. NULL encryption is the default, so that intermediate devices on your network will be able to inspect the communications, if that is required. As you can with the hashing algorithm, you can change the encryption scheme if you like.

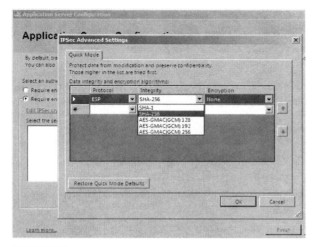

FIGURE 5-16

When you've chosen the appropriate settings, click Generate Policies, as shown in Figure 5-17, and GPO objects and settings are configured by the wizard. After that happens, a button is available to let you deploy the GPOs (the Forefront UAG Wizard does this for you, but you also have the option to do it yourself, if you prefer). Remember to Activate the configuration after you've deployed the GPOs; I often forget to do this and then have to troubleshoot the problem because my connectivity doesn't work.

FIGURE 5-17

Administrator's Punch List

- The infrastructure tunnels allow the DirectAccess client to access management and infrastructure servers before the user logs on; infrastructure tunnel authentication is performed via computer certificate and computer account (NTLMv2) authentication.

- The intranet tunnels are established after the user logs on and enable the user to access all resources on the intranet that the user is authorized to access; intranet tunnel authorization is performed via computer certificate and user account (Kerberos) authentication.

- Both DirectAccess tunnels use AES encryption to provide privacy over the Internet.

- IPv6 transition technologies (Teredo, 6to4, and IP-HTTPS) allow the DirectAccess client to send IPv6 messages over the IPv4 Internet.

- ISATAP can be used on intranets that are not running a native IPv6 infrastructure to tunnel IPv6 messages over an IPv4 intranet architecture.

- The DirectAccess client always uses IPv6 to communicate with the Forefront UAG DirectAccess server.

- Forefront UAG includes NAT64/DNS64 that allows the Forefront UAG DirectAccess server to forward IPv6 messages from the DirectAccess clients to IPv4-only servers on the intranet.

- DirectAccess clients send DNS queries to the DNS64 services on the Forefront UAG DirectAccess server to resolve names on the intranet.

- The Name Resolution Policy Table (NRPT) is a method of DNS routing that allows the DirectAccess client to send queries for names on the intranet to the DNS64 services on the Forefront UAG DirectAccess server.

- The Forefront UAG DirectAccess server and DirectAccess clients must be domain members, although they do not need to be members of the same domain or forest.

- A PKI infrastructure is required to assign certificates to the Network Location Server, the DirectAccess server, DirectAccess clients, and the IP-HTTPS listener on the Forefront UAG DirectAccess server.

- Network location servers are used by DirectAccess clients to determine if they are on the intranet. If the DirectAccess client cannot establish an SSL connection to a Network Location Server, then it determines that it is off the intranet and leaves the NRPT enabled.

- For IP-HTTPS connections, the CRL of the CA that issued the IP-HTTPS certificate must be available to DirectAccess clients on the Internet.

- Forefront UAG DirectAccess servers include integrated support for NAP.

- Forefront UAG DirectAccess server includes integrated support for smart card two-factor authentication.

- DirectAccess clients are considered to be more secure than typical remote access VPN clients because the DirectAccess clients are always under corporate IT command and control.

- Split tunneling is enabled by default for DirectAccess clients. Split tunneling can be disabled by enabling the "Force Tunneling" configuration on the DirectAccess clients.